THE ESSENTIAL

SURVIVAL
HANDBOOK

This is a Carlton Book

Text and Design © Carlton Books Limited 2002

First published in 2002 by Carlton Books

10 9 8 7 6 5 4 3 2 1

A CIP catalogue record for this book is available from the British Library.

ISBN: 1 84222 669-X

Executive Editor: Vanessa Daubney
Project Art Director: Darren Jordan
Design: Vaseem Bhatti
Illustrations: Peter Liddiard
Jacket Design: Steve Lynn
Picture research: Marc Glanville
Production: Sarah Corteel

Printed and bound in Great Britain

THE ESSENTIAL
SURVIVAL
HANDBOOK

Ken Griffiths

CARLTON
BOOKS

Dedication

To my wife Alexandra and my girls Kelly, Emily and Caroline.

Acknowledgements

To the British Army, for paying me to train and giving me the opportunity to experience what it's like to survive armed conflict and to teach others to survive; Sergeant Major Eddie McGee, for the times we spent together and the experience I gained from him; The Royal Geographical Society, for the hours I have spent in the map-room planning my expeditions; Captain Jonathon Barrington-Brookes-Ford, for his support loyalty and the training we endured together; Keele University's Education Department, for employing me to teach and study the effects of survival on the students who attended the lectures and ground training; The Academy of Experts, Gray's Inn London, for their extensive training in mediation and negotiation; Sergeant Major Mike Beaman, for his support; Sergeant Major Brian Harding (Chick), for the close protection and evasive driving training.

Contents

PART 1
Mind Set To Win

1. The Psychology of Survival

Over recent years the terms 'survival', 'survivalism' and 'survivalist' have been closely linked with gun-toting, muscle-bound machismo figures, misunderstood rogue soldiers and serving military special forces personnel trained to penetrate deep into enemy territory. The media hype surrounding these types of characters has been further enhanced by the writings of former and currently serving military survival instructors. Given this, it's sometimes hard to understand how we mere mortals could ever survive! In fact, the truth is that very ordinary people have accomplished the vast majority of successful fights for survival against the odds. And why not? After all, we are survivors; every day of our lives is one of survival. Some of us survive the crime-ridden streets of major cities, others the remote jungles of Papua New Guinea. The difference is the day-to-day severity of the fight and our knowledge of the area in which we live. Throughout our lives we develop the skills needed to cope with our changing environment. Many of us expand this knowledge to enable us to cope with, and live and work in, a wide variety of climatic, geographical and man-made extremes. The difficulty arises when we are forced to survive in environments that we are not mentally, emotionally or physically prepared for. And yet, given a group of individuals in the same dangerous, life-threatening situation, without adequate knowledge or training some will live through whilst others die. Political prisoners who have been subjected to extreme torture violence, starvation and appalling conditions, suffering severe injuries and disease have lived whilst others with relatively minor ailments have given up and died. It has to be the case that the latter group lost their will to survive.

Over the years, there have been many reported incidents of outstanding personal courage that have demonstrated man's will to survive against all the odds. One particular act that I believe underpins this, is the true account of a lone working farmer who, having had his arm severed in agricultural machinery, had the presence of mind to realize that if he collapsed he would not survive. In that moment of logical decision he carried his severed arm a considerable distance to effect a self-rescue and thereby saved his own life.

Experiences such as this are proof that survivors are not made, and that training alone is not sufficient to win the fight: mental attitude is more important! I have seen the biggest and hardest crumble under the pressure of simulated and actual survival encounters, and then watched as the stereotypical weaklings have fought and won to gain a firm grip of the situation and their existence.

An appropriate definition of the word 'survive' is to fight, to live on when all help has gone. Obviously this is survival in its most extreme form. Fortunately, not many of us will ever be in this position. In the majority of cases the survival fight lasts only as long as it takes for help to arrive. The difficulty is having the courage, coupled with the will to stay alive long enough either to await the arrival of rescuers or to effect a self-rescue. In both cases, the survival priorities are the same and can be listed in order of priority as:

- **PROTECTION**
- **LOCATION**
- **WATER**
- **FOOD.**

During the course of this book, all of these priorities will be discussed in detail along with many more aspects of survival and personal safety.

Having the theoretical knowledge of survival and safety techniques will be a benefit to you and those around you if you are ever faced with a life- threatening situation. Add to this some field training and specific experience, and your ability will be greatly enhanced and your chances of survival correspondingly higher.

When faced with a potential survival situation, it is most important that you quickly recognize the immediate dangers and how to avoid or control them effectively, and the long-term effects and potential dangers that can be set in motion by poor judgement at this most crucial stage.

Other than injury, wind, wet and cold account for the majority of deaths in the survival situation. Given this, it is obvious that the survivor's first priority will be to protect against these conditions and any other adverse weather that is or will become hazardous. The human body has the capability to produce its own heat. The problem is that body heat is quickly removed by wind. This cooling effect is known as the wind chill (see *Surviving Cold*), and becomes more rapid when the body is wet. Protection from hypothermia (an abnormally low body temperature resulting in death) is paramount in these conditions.

The sun's strong rays can take the body heat to a degree that will induce death. Although the effects are not as rapid as with hypothermia, the overall effect can be just as dangerous. In hot climates your protection will be to keep physical activities to a minimum during the hottest part of the day and find shelter from the sun's rays, preferably in a well-ventilated position. The need for clean drinking water is obvious, and will be dealt with later in the Water section.

Obviously, your physical condition will have an effect on your efficiency, but as I have already indicated, a positive psychological approach will keep you alive even though you may have severe injuries. It goes without saying that a good knowledge of first aid will be a great advantage.

A lack of knowledge in the skills you need to survive will inevitably lead to an overall lack of confidence. A lack of confidence can lead to a state of panic, and panic is one of the most dangerous and life-threatening responses there is. Once a person is gripped by panic, logic and sensible thought are often replaced by illogical and irresponsible actions. Even a little knowledge goes a long way in averting panic and fear.

From the very beginning, take control of yourself. Have the confidence to fight. Your mind will naturally want you to survive, and in the sub-conscious there is a wealth of brainpower to help you to develop the **will to survive.** Without this belief, you will surely die. The problem is that you have probably never consciously accessed this wealth of brainpower, and you may work against it by convincing yourself that you can't survive or win!

Be sure that you set your mind to 'win' mode. You can win, you can survive; other people do, and so can you!

Developing the **will to survive** is the first step in defeating the natural enemies of wind, cold, wet and sun. From here on, the struggle is with yourself!

Once you have mastered the will to survive, you will find that the aids to your survival will be your inner strength (often much stronger in females), your knowledge, the equipment you have or can find or manufacture, and your psychological approach (which is greatly enhanced by a sense of humour).

Never give up! Never let anyone or anything get the better of you! Never think you can't: know that you can!

2. The Psychology of Self-Defence

Physical violence and aggression are not someone else's problem: they can and do affect all of us. The perpetrators of these types of crimes against the person are indiscriminate in their selection of targets. The young, the old, male, female, healthy, disabled, black, white – they're all the same to the person who chooses violence in order to gain control and power over others.

We all have a right to enjoy our lives in freedom, free from oppression. The problem is that not everyone adheres to these principles, and some take great pleasure in stripping others of these basic rights. Every day of our lives there is the potential for us to meet and have to deal with violence and aggression. For the most part, we manage to deal with this by diffusing the situation, by using our communication skills to navigate through the aggressor's mind until we meet his social conscience (everyone has one – it's just that some are very distorted and often shaped by the person's own early violent life events). Once we find the aggressor's switch, our communication skills can either make the matter worse or work to turn the aggression off – or at least tone it down enough to move the situation away from a violent act. All things being equal, we achieve this by self-confidence. If we show a lack of confidence in our negotiations, then we risk giving the aggressor a signal of our uncertainty and vulnerability. Once this happens, the negotiation is one-sided: his! Whereas if we can continue to show confidence, we can often avoid physical confrontation. Having good communication skills often moves the interaction from a physical confrontation to a verbal settlement (see Section Three: *Effective Communication*).

When the talking stops, or when you are stopped from talking, you may then have to resort to violence. Unfortunately, in life you can't avoid man: the aggressor, the hunter, and very often the hunter of man! Because of this, there are times when you have to fight back.

In the daily fight for survival, you may well be confronted by an aggressive and violent person who is intent on causing you damage or even killing you. Physical violence is not pleasant, but neither is it unstoppable. As with all aspects of personal safety and survival, much depends on your ability to quickly change the way you think and deal with the situation. Generally the fear of an attack is often worse than the attack itself. Once you have made the decision to fight – or have had the decision forced upon you – you must be absolutely determined to win, and that means being as ruthless as you can. Begin now to remove the sporting mentality: aim to stop the aggressor. It sounds extreme, I know, but if someone is willing to act violently towards you, you must conquer your own feelings of compassion and your distaste of violence. When you fight, fight for your life with all your inner strength.

Be absolutely resolute when you are faced with having to defend yourself or someone else against the possibility of an attack or an actual attack. Once the action starts, refuse to accept defeat and work hard to achieve victory. Accept no rules in your combat, and revert to a brutality to match that of your aggressor: you may be dealing with a life-threatening situation, and as such there is no place for scruples. The second you hesitate, the aggressor will take the initiative, and that is very likely to result in your demise.

One of the problems with the average law-abiding person is that they fear the consequence of this type of action. Throughout their lives they have been taught to respect the law and to respect other people. That's all well and good if you are dealing with a compassionate, normal-thinking decent individual. But for anyone to use extreme violence, they clearly do not fit into this category.

If you are confronted with violence, you do have the right to defend yourself against an attack as long as you can demonstrate that you used reasonable force. The force you use must not be excessive, but if you are faced with someone intent on killing you, it is reasonable to stop them by killing them first!

Meeting aggression and violence with aggression and violence is not something that comes easily to most people. As well as the physical effect of having to fight for your life and beat your opponent, there is the psychological effect. In most cases, this damage goes on long after the body has repaired. Console yourself with the thought that you would not have resorted to the crudeness of violence if the aggressor had not forced you into it. Post-trauma stress is a well-known condition, and there are excellent counselling courses available if you think you need some support afterwards.

The real test is this: if you can put your hand on your heart and swear that you acted in self-defence, and that you did what you had to do to stop yourself and/or those around you from getting hurt or even to prevent loss of life, then you have nothing to feel guilty about.

3. Effective Communication

Communication is the way in which we exchange information, ideas and our feelings. We do this in a number of ways. We can write a book, compile a letter, use television, e-mail, the telephone or a video link. All of these are 'long-arm' communication tools. In the survival situation, you will be face to face with your aggressor: your opponent. You may think that your first words will be the beginning of your communication with him, but you would be quite wrong. At the very moment of the first glimpse, communication has already started without a word being spoken. Through the eyes, the figure and facial features of the person are transmitted to the brain; within a millisecond, the picture joins that section of the brain that holds the schema of all the people you have met, seen and have had described to you. Without you realizing it, your body is reacting – your body language is already communicating with the other person. You may never have met this person before, but he could fit a particular negative stereotype that you already have. He may be dressed in a way that shows his religious or political beliefs, or he may remind you of a person who has posed a threat to you in the past. Likewise, he will have already begun analysing you in the same way. Understanding the way in which non-verbal communication works and adapting this may be the edge you need in order to interact verbally with a possible attacker or terrorist without antagonizing them or making yourself a target. When speech does begin, the speaker's tone of voice is another signal that can enhance or diminish rapport.

Non-verbal communication accounts for between 55% and 90% of everyday conversation. How the aggressor reacts to you will be greatly influenced by your body language and your tone of voice. Understanding the signs and being able to read them quickly will help you to react in a positive way and hopefully turn a violent confrontation into a two-way conversation.

When faced with the prospect of violence, the human body and mind react to protect and prepare either to stay and fight or to run away. It's very difficult to control this innate reaction, and equally difficult to stop yourself from reacting long enough to make a proper appraisal and adopt the most appropriate response. Being able to communicate effectively in these situations will help you to take control and lessen the risk of a physically violent outcome.

Being assertive

If you are able to get your point across, and at the same time you can allow the other person to put their point of view to you without either party feeling threatened, then you have achieved the fundamental process of assertive communication. If your body language and tone of voice present themselves as aggressive, then this will be read by your opponent as you allowing yourself the right of expression whilst denying them their right to express themselves. This type of interaction can only result in an escalation of aggression and ultimately violence. Remember: in the survival situation your first priority has to be protection, and that means diverting and avoiding violence at all costs.

The key is to engineer your interaction with your opponent to the point where you and they have a feeling of mutual respect (even if you don't actually respect them!).

During my mediation and negotiation training, I was introduced to a concept where the mutual respect between hostage and captor develops to the point of virtual collusion. Known as the Stockholm syndrome, it describes the tendency for the hostage to actually protect the captor! I've witnessed a similar situation with long-term undercover operators who have formed close bonds with the criminals and terrorists they have been observing. As a result of this relationship, they have become a danger to their colleagues and have jeopardized whole operations.

Obviously, there are thousands of non-verbal indicators that can be learned and observed to give you an indication of the true feelings of your opponent. The following is a sample of the most common ones to watch for and to avoid giving out.

- The head tilted down is an indication that the person is unsure.

  YOU: The last thing you need is for your opponent to be given a signal that tells them that you are unsure. You must always present yourself as being confident and in control.

  THEM: Once you recognize this signal, you must have touched a vulnerable spot. Use the same line of conversation carefully to keep your opponent on their back foot: they are obviously struggling.

- Hand clenched as a fist across the chest is a sure sign of an unfriendly person.

  YOU: If you are trying to enter into a productive stage of communication, it may well be to your disadvantage to display your hostility to the other side.

  THEM: Be very careful, this person will need handling with great care. They are clearly hostile and are not on the same playing field as you. If at all possible, keep out of their way. If you have to interact, give them room to be a little hostile, and be ready to use your assertive skills to stop them from overstepping their mark. In a hostage or terrorist situation, make plans to eliminate this person first if there is a likelihood of you becoming a target.

- The jabbing of fingers during verbal communication shows that the person is becoming aggressive; if the jabbing escalates, then they are becoming more agitated.

  YOU: This gesture can inflame the situation and enrage your opponent. Keep your fingers to yourself!

  THEM: Clearly whatever is happening in the communication, it is inflaming the situation, not diffusing it. Use your skills to calm the situation before it gets out of hand.

In many situations, you may be able to avert aggressive or violent action by using the communication skill of assertiveness. It is worth pointing out here that many people confuse assertiveness with aggression: the two are absolutely different. Aggressive conversation works on the premise that the aggressor has more rights than the person they are communicating with, whereas assertive communication is about putting your point across with the understanding that the other person has a right to their opinion and point of view.

When people communicate in this way, then the conversation is a two-way exchange and a lot of dialogue can take place; this will often diffuse a potentially aggressive and violent interaction. In essence, everyone has the right to:

- State their needs and to ask for what they want
- Set their personal priorities
- Be treated with respect and dignity
- Express their feelings, opinions and beliefs
- Have the opportunity to agree, disagree and to say 'yes' and 'no'
- Be seen and treated as an equal
- Have the opportunity to change their minds without being ridiculed or seen as weakening
- Be allowed to make mistakes and to re-think their position
- Let it be known that they do not understand and to have the whole matter or certain points properly and fully explained
- State their beliefs without feeling that they have to have the other person's approval
- Make decisions for themselves
- Accept or not accept that they are responsible for solving other people's problems

Assertive communication is an enabling device, a psychological approach that gives the parties the room to manoeuvre without feeling that they are seen as weaker than the person they are communicating with.

When the balance of communication is equal, then negative and unpredictable emotions such as anger and fear can be alleviated and replaced by constructive and positive responses. Clearly, when this point has been reached, then there is the opportunity to negotiate properly and effectively move away from aggression and violence.

4. Developing Awareness

People often say that they know when something bad is going to happen well before it actually does, or that they can spot a person who is a threat or about to commit a crime. Some would say that these people are psychic. I actually believe that they are more likely to have developed a sense of security and are subconsciously monitoring the environment they are in and the people they meet. It doesn't really matter what view you hold; it is the case that people do have a sense of danger and an internal warning mechanism. Always trust and act on your own feelings and instincts.

You can help to develop your overall awareness by taking more notice of your surroundings and the people you encounter. If you are travelling, take the time to find out about the geography, geology, natural faults and weather patterns before you go. By doing this you will not be so surprised if you encounter an earthquake or sudden typhoon.

In hotels and other buildings in which you may be staying, look around to find the most appropriate escape route in the event of a fire or disaster. If you are in a high-rise building where your only means of escape is by following the signed emergency exits, you should walk the escape route and make sure that you know how to open the doors and negotiate other hazards. Removing any obstructions that you find along the way may well save your life. If you find that there is no realistic way of exiting to safety, ask to be moved to a ground-floor room. Check that the windows and doors open easily. Likewise, make sure that you can secure yourself in your room if there is a possibility of a violent encounter. Wherever you stay, always make sure that you have an escape route and a safe place to hide.

Wherever you are, whatever you are doing, be aware of the possible dangers of the place and its people. Make every effort to organize yourself, your room and your vehicles to give you the upper hand in an emergency. It may be that you are inadvertently leaving weapons around for a chance attacker to use. An example of this would be knives left on display in kitchens overnight. Imagine you are a burglar and have been surprised by the house occupants. You are in the kitchen, where an assortment of knives is on display! It's not difficult to see what the result might be.

Be aware, stay alive!

PART 2
Protection

5. Shelters and Shelter Building

A shelter is an object, position or location that provides an area of cover or protection from adverse weather, the elements or some danger – whether imagined or real. As well as fulfilling the obvious role of providing physical protection, well-made shelters should offer the occupants as comfortable and as safe an environment as possible. This is difficult to achieve, especially in a hurriedly constructed makeshift shelter. Nevertheless you should aim to build a temporary dwelling that you can sleep in. In the survival situation, you will be surprised at how quickly you become tired and how much physical and mental effort is needed to carry out even the simplest task. Sleep rests the body and mind; its rejuvenating power will re-energize you and increase your physical and psychological strength. The more sleep you get, the better you will feel. Unfortunately, sleeping in survival situations is not easy. One of the ways of dealing with this is to sleep when you are tired, and to forget about your normal day-to-day habit of going to bed to sleep and rising at regular times. Catnapping helps you to cope in hostile situations and environments, as well as conserving your energy.

Over the years, when I have undergone survival training, and on the few occasions on which I have been forced to adopt the survival mode, I have found that in the early stages it is easier to gain quality sleep during daylight hours than when it is dark. There is no problem with this, as long as you have carried out the necessary work to sustain yourself. Trying to sleep at night in wet and cold conditions can quickly sap your inner strength. If you cannot sleep, you may as well stay awake and tend the fire. If you do this, you will keep relatively warm and occupied and probably catnap quite a lot, which will help to conserve your energy.

The chances are that you will have arrived at your location by some form of transport. It may well be worthwhile utilizing any vehicles, or whatever is left of them, as the foundation for your shelter. Having said that, it is not always the best policy to use vehicles as shelters, as in most cases they are made of metal and can act as a refrigerator in cold weather and an oven when it is hot. It is often better to construct your shelter using a mixture of vehicle panels and interior fittings, along with any local shelter-building materials you can find. If you do decide to utilize a vehicle, make sure that it is free from any hazard such as leaking fuel and is not placed in a precarious position. In deciding whether or not to stay with and make use of any wreckage, you have to consider whether or not you want to be found. It may be the case that you are in a politically hostile and dangerous place and do not want to be found by the locals – in which case you would be well advised to move away from any wreckage or broken-down vehicles, as these can easily be spotted. Obviously, if you do want to be found, staying nearby will help any search-and-rescue attempt.

In general terms, the type of shelter you use or construct will be determined by:

- The elements from which you need to be protected
- Your geographical location
- Any shelter-building materials you have arrived with, and/or local vegetation and geological features
- The length of time for which you anticipate staying, or are likely to stay – this can vary immensely, and will be determined by a variety of factors that will be discussed in the *Search-and-Rescue* section.
- Whether or not you wish to be seen or found
- The number of people in the party and their level of ability, physical and psychological fitness, and injuries or the likelihood of further injuries.

When faced with a survival situation that requires you to make a shelter, your first consideration should be to choose a suitable site. This is all well and good if it is a nice sunny day and you have plenty of time to make your choice, but in reality your first shelter may merely be a hurriedly constructed windbreak using a hollow in the ground or at the foot of a natural windbreak such as thick, low vegetation.

I have been in situations where I have had to find a shelter in the dead of night, in the cold and with rain lashing down. Having experienced these conditions, I can confirm that it is extremely difficult to find the best location, and you may well have to make do with whatever you can find quickly to offer you some immediate protection from the elements and to give you the opportunity to gather your thoughts.

If the area in which you find yourself is at high altitude, ideally you should make every effort to move lower down. By doing this you will be less exposed, which reduces the risk of freezing conditions. However, unless you are absolutely sure that you are capable of completing the move and that it is safe to do so, stay where you are until you can properly plan your descent. In any event, avoid following streams and rivers, as these tend to find the quickest route down a hill or mountain – which is usually over the edge of a cliff!

When you do have a chance to study your surroundings properly, take a close look at the geology. In limestone areas and rocky shorelines, you are more likely to find caves. These can make excellent shelters, but you should be aware that they have probably been formed by the constant action of water either from incoming tides or from underground rivers, and therefore they will have a tendency to flood.

I have spent a lot of time living and working in cave systems – sometimes for long periods lasting many days – without seeing any natural light. They can be very difficult to heat, are usually hard and uncomfortable environments and, although they appear completely dry, they can flood in seconds without warning.

If you do decide on a cave, choose wisely and keep in mind that people and water do not usually mix! Also, many caves are already home to animals and insects – especially bats, which, when roosting, tend to let their droppings build up on the cave floor in layers that can be quite deep; when dry, they form a dense powder that, once disturbed, fills the cave with a mist of toxic particles; when wet, they are the home of millions of gruesome insects. All of this adds up to a very unhealthy place to rest your weary head.

Other rock formations and outcrops can also offer the basis of a decent shelter. Sedimentary rocks such as sandstones and grits are often eroded and weathered, and have fissures and hollows that offer good protection. Most of these features have been made by prevailing winds and weather, so be sure that you make your choice with the elements in mind. Rocks

CAVE DWELLING

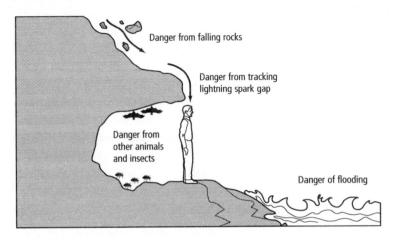

Caves can make quick and adequate shelters. although they are difficult to heat, have very hard and uncomfortable surfaces, can flood without warning and have some very nasty inhabitants!

OVERHANGING ROCK SHELTER

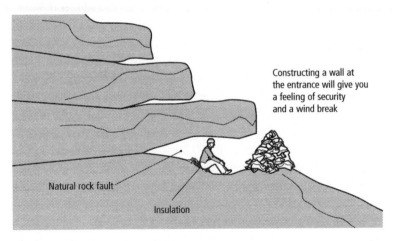

Using the rock's natural faults as a basis from which to build your shelter can be a very effective way of quickly establishing and consolidating your position.

have a habit of breaking off from time to time – especially when they are exposed to extreme heat during the day and freezing conditions at night. If your chosen site is in the shadow of high rocks, use natural sturdy overhangs as a roof protection from falling fragments or sliding scree. If you cannot find adequate protection, build your shelter far enough away to avoid any potential rock-falls.

Another potential hazard involves igneous rocks such as granite. Granites are harder than sedimentary rocks. Outcrops usually contain horizontal cracks and joints formed during the rock's cooling period and expanded by thousands of years of local erosion. These can be the foundation of your shelter. However, these types of rock are often highly magnetized, and can distort the readings on navigation instruments.

Woodland areas should provide you with an ample supply of materials for your shelter, but there are some fundamental problems you should be aware of. Trees can and do rot; consequently they become extremely unstable, and can shed parts as small as twigs or as large as huge boughs. In the worst case, the whole lot can come down without any prior warning. Rotten trees and vegetation also harbour a great deal of insect life, which can prove to be both unpleasant and even dangerous if disturbed during shelter construction.

In the early 1980s, I spent some time in the Falkland Islands. On one occasion in the Douglas area, I disturbed the ground vegetation as I constructed my shelter. Within seconds I was covered in flea-like insects – in fact, the whole of the shelter was crawling with these tiny pests. In such circumstances, there is nothing you can do other than to accept them and get on with the task in hand.

Using a tree trunk as the centre pole of your shelter may seem like a good idea – and it can be, as long as you construct the shelter in the knowledge that tree trunks move in windy conditions, and that when it rains, water uses the trunk as a route to the ground. In very heavy rain, the amount of water rushing down can resemble a gutter downpipe. An exception to this is when there is a heavy fall of snow on evergreens such as spruce. I have spent many a comfortable – and, dare I say, pleasant – night, sheltering in the relative calm of a Norwegian forest protected by the natural shelter beneath a snow-covered tree.

Taking refuge in the boughs of trees and constructing a Tarzan-type tree hut may seem a good idea, but in reality trees are living things and therefore growing and constantly moving and bending with the wind. Dead timber soon becomes weak and is unsafe to use for shelter building. It may seem fine when you construct the frame for your shelter, but it becomes very unstable with the weight of the shelter covering, especially when the covering is further weighed down by rain water or a heavy fall of snow. Whenever possible, use only fresh, green, flexible timber for shelter frame construction.

One last tree hazard that needs to be thought about is the lone tree. Lightning likes to find earth, and chooses to do this by finding the most convenient conductor. If there are no buildings, communication masts, wreckage or umbrellas, it will find a tree instead.

You can usually feel the build-up to an electric storm. The air around you somehow feels heavier – thicker even. Look up into the sky, and you are likely to see huge anvil-shaped clouds known as cumulonimbus, which form as a cold weather-front passes. In exposed situations, you can also often experience a tingling feeling. Once you see a flash of lightning, count the seconds until you hear the thunder. Three seconds equates to approximately one kilometre, four to a mile. By doing this, you can work out how far away the lightning is and how much time you have to move to a safe area. If you are on an exposed ridge, you really need to move down – you should do this, even when the storm is upon you. In high terrain the lightning adopts a pattern of closer strikes as it approaches a mountain. Moving over the mountain, the frequency of strikes reduces. If you can get into the strikes' shadow, the chances of being hit are very much reduced. If you have not prepared a decent shelter or found a large cave that you can get right back into, it is safer if you sit in open country and use luggage, thick vegetation, a coiled rope or something you can find to sit on as insulation.

I have had the experience of being in the middle of an electric storm on an Albanian mountainside, with lightning striking and snapping huge fir trees as though they were nothing more than match-sticks – awe-inspiring and excitingly dangerous, but not for the faint-hearted or distressed survivor.

After the storm, there may well be a number of felled trees that can be organized to form a very effective shelter.

As with woodland areas, jungles should offer you plenty of shelter-building materials. I say 'should', because to the uninitiated the word *jungle* evokes a picture of tropical forests filled with lush vegetation, when in reality the amount and type of vegetation really depend on the altitude. In fact, jungles can range from lush greenery to large areas of open scrubland. For the most part though, the jungle environment consists of a great abundance of competing vegetation. In their natural, primary state, jungles will have a prolific growth of tall, straight trees that rise

TREE BIVOUAC

Using the natural cover of a felled tree's foliage, and organizing it to form a barrier between you and the outside world, can turn a disaster into a decent dwelling.

pole-like from the jungle floor for 60 metres (180 feet) or more before their branches spread and interlock with those of neighbouring trees. Rich, green foliage adorns the whole to form a dense canopy that effectively blocks out sunlight. Not surprisingly, very little grows beneath the canopy so the majority of wildlife and insects live in the trees: the result is that travel through primary jungle is relatively easy. Unfortunately, man tends to change his environment to suit his needs, and the jungle is no exception. As a result, many of the primary jungle trees have been destroyed – usually by fire as a way of clearing areas that are then planted with crops by local tribes. Thousands of years of this practice – along with occasional blanket bombing in war zones – have left very little primary jungle. Although in many cases man's use of the cleared land is short-lived, the jungle floor is exposed to sunlight, and fast-growing vegetation soon establishes itself – making it virtually impossible for the tall trees to grow back. This secondary jungle is very dense, is home to a great deal of insect and animal life, and is extremely difficult to move through.

Shelters will vary depending on the type of jungle you are presented with. Nevertheless you should always construct a lying area that is off the ground, as millions of insects live in the layers of dead and decaying vegetation that make up a typical jungle floor; torrential rain can also flood the ground.

Moorland consists of peaty soil covered with heather and coarse grasses with occasional bracken and a dense covering of mosses. There is very little cover above knee height, so you are forced to keep your shelter low to the ground. Peat has a tendency to act like a sponge, and holds a great deal of water. Once you disturb it by breaking the surface – by digging, for example, – the hole soon fills with brackish brown water (which is often very smelly). Shelter construction in this type of terrain can be very testing, but if you keep to the basic rule that all you need to do is protect yourself from the cold, the rain and wind, you can achieve this by keeping the shelter low, slightly off the ground and comfortably small.

If you have the time and tools, you can construct a decent shelter by stacking blocks of peat to form a tunnel and using local vegetation to form the roof. Quite often, snow will be lying on higher moorland areas, and you can use it to cover the roof by throwing it over the existing roof supports and thatching.

Most people will understand the concept of using snow to form an *igloo* – as the Eskimo's dome-shaped shelter is universally known. The snow used in this type of shelter is very compacted, and is expertly cut using a long saw/knife. If the snow is of the right texture, and you have the means and the time to cut it, and you can stand hard work, you can make a very comfortable shelter.

No matter what type of snow shelter you construct, you will find the task difficult and physically demanding; having a selection of digging and cutting tools will certainly help. However, it's possible to construct a basic shelter using nothing more than your hands.

A firm drift of snow or a slope will make construction easier, as you can use this type of feature to burrow into. You need to keep your shelter small so that you do not lose heat once you are inside. The entrance should likewise be kept as small as possible, leaving just enough room to squeeze in and out. A small opening makes it much easier to seal from the inside, keeping the weather out. Snow is a relatively good insulator, and will certainly keep the wind off; in fact, the temperature inside a well-constructed snow shelter can be many degrees higher than the outside temperature. Heat rises, so consequently cool air falls. To gain the best benefit from this, you need to construct a shelf to sit or lie on with a cold air trough well below; obviously, you will have to insulate yourself from

SNOW HOLE

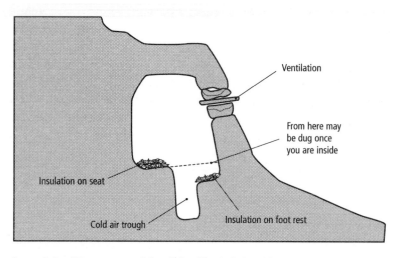

Ventilation

From here may
be dug once
you are inside

Insulation on seat

Cold air trough

Insulation on foot rest

A snow hole will keep you out of the wind and is relatively quick to construct. As time goes by, you can make it a little more comfortable by expanding it into a snow cave.

SNOW CAVE

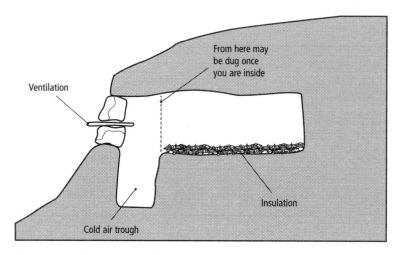

From here may
be dug once
you are inside

Ventilation

Insulation

Cold air trough

the snow by using any vegetation you can find, or extra clothing that you may have with you to place between you and the cold surface. Another advantage of the trough is that it will act as a drain. Body heat in snow shelters begins to melt a thin layer of snow. By constructing the shelter in a dome fashion, the melt water clings to the surface and runs down the walls, effectively stopping any drips. The water then collects in the trough and freezes. If there is a persistent drip, pushing snow onto it will stop it.

On deep, flat snow you may have to resort to a trench – it's not as effective as a snow cave in the first place, but it will get you out of the wind and weather quickly. The roof is the main problem; if you can cut slabs of snow or ice, you can use these to construct a pitched roof. Other than this, you may be able to use branches from trees or other vegetation to build the roof. Packing the frame with snow will further insulate and seal it. Make sure that the frame can support the weight of the covering. If you are forced to stay in the shelter for any length of time, you can develop it to incorporate a cave.

SNOW TRENCH AND ALTERNATIVE

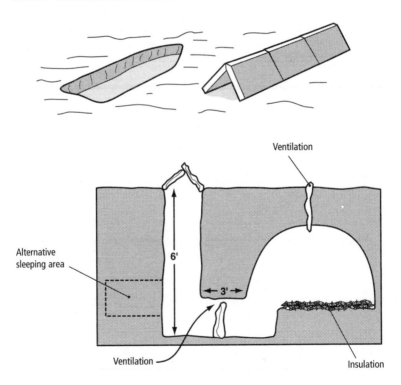

A simple snow trench may be the only shelter you need in an emergency. As you consolidate your position, you can improve on the basic design.

In areas of loose, shallow snow, you may have to resort to gathering it up to form a soft snow mound. The best way of doing this is to begin by rolling three giant snowballs and pushing them together. Follow this by gathering soft snow and cover the three balls to form the mound. The snow will soon consolidate, and then you can burrow into it to form a decent shelter.

Deserts

When most people think of a desert, they often have an image of white soft sand, nomadic tribes travelling on camels, and lush oases. In fact, the term 'desert' means a region that is devoid or virtually devoid of vegetation – usually because of a lack of water. But not always: there are many deserts that are areas of frozen wasteland. Around one fifth of the Earth's surface is described as desert and the largest areas surround the Persian Gulf and the Red Sea.

In the survival situation it is generally better to stay in one place and to make the most of the resources you can find locally; movement on foot is both difficult and dangerous. Desert sand is not the same as that found on beaches: it is hard, sharp and angular, and permeates everything you have – as well as finding its way into every orifice of the human body. It is best to take refuge by day in a large shelter that is constructed to offer as much shade as possible with a flow of fresh air. At night the shelter should be capable of being closed down tightly and made small enough to conserve heat, as night-time temperatures in the desert often drop well below freezing. Broken-down or wrecked vehicles may seem like good shelter, but the metal becomes incredibly hot and acts like an oven, burning flesh if it is touched and cooking bodies within. Seeking shade under the vehicle should also be avoided, as the weight often makes it sink in soft sand.

Sand is a difficult medium to use in shelter building. Tunnelling is dangerous, and a scrape or hollow is safer as the basis. A piece of wreckage can be used as a roof, and covering it with sand helps to insulate it slightly, keeping the shelter a little cooler during the day and helping to retain some heat for the cold night.

General shelter-building points

The position of your shelter will have a significant bearing on its effectiveness. As I have already stated, you may not be in a position or have the time to choose a decent site properly. However, once the initial trauma is over, you should consider whether you are likely to be rescued sooner or later. Even if you consider that your rescuers will be along soon, you should still make an effort to work on your shelter and make it a little more comfortable and weatherproof. The following is a list of pointers that apply in the majority of shelters and shelter-building techniques.

- If at all possible, get down to a lower site and avoid exposed ridges
- Select a site on level ground and clear it of debris and loose rocks
- Keep off damp ground
- Keep away from lone trees, and any other feature that is prone to a lightning strike or tracking of lightning
- Check above you to ensure that you are not going to be exposed to falling rocks, branches, and other hazards
- Keep well away from dead and rotting vegetation, and other features that harbour insects and their nests
- Although you need water to survive, constructing a shelter close to water (especially swamps and marshes) may expose you to biting insects; it's often better to walk a little way to get your water, than to be too close
- Do not site your shelter in a dry gully, which could flood without warning, but site your shelter out of the prevailing wind
- Use strong, fresh, supple timber as the shelter's main frame
- Pay particular attention to weatherproofing
- In cold climates, keep your shelter small to conserve heat, and in hot climates make it large enough to encourage shade and draughts; make sure that you can close it down to a smaller size for the cold nights
- A small shelter is quicker to construct, uses fewer materials and is easier to keep warm
- In all shelters, make sure that there is a good supply of fresh air; this is especially important with snow shelters
- Unless you do not want to be found in the particular area of your survival encounter, make sure that your shelter is well marked, and can be seen from the air and from a long distance away
- Construct an entrance that is easy to close yet large enough to be able to get in and out of quickly in an emergency
- Use plenty of insulation material between you and the ground. The more insulation you can use the better.

6. Surviving in Cold Climates

Man's urge to survive is one of the strongest animal instincts we possess. There is no greater test of this than survival in freezing conditions when the body becomes numb with cold. In such conditions there is an enormous amount of personal stress that constantly tests the mind and body; problems that would normally mean nothing become massive. Survivors in these conditions often experience feelings of isolation and deep depression, resulting in great mood swings that have the effect of undermining any efficiency. Even in a group, these feelings prevail, and can often change an effective team into a bunch of individuals working in opposition to one another. A sense of humour is a very important survival tool in all situations, but in the cold it is absolutely vital to maintain a sense of *camaraderie* and positive thought – all of which fosters that much-needed will to survive.

One of the most important human attributes for the survivor is the body's ability to change its functions to cope in differing environments. After a period of acclimatization the survivor can cope better with cold and harsh conditions. It has already been pointed out that protection is the first survival priority; in cold climates, this protection allows the survivor vital time to begin the acclimatization process. In time, the body does have the capacity to produce extra fat that forms protective layers: keeping as warm as possible is therefore vital.

The body fights cold by producing its own heat, which it does by converting food into heat energy. The more food you have, the bigger the increases in body heat. This heat is transported to the vital organs and muscles by the body's blood. In extreme cold, keeping the muscles moving will force the blood into the body's extremities, effectively reducing the risk of frostbite.

As the cold air temperature cools the outer body, it sends a signal to the brain. In turn, the brain, believing that there is the possibility of a rapid cooling of the body core, begins the process of inner protection. The blood flow is changed, cutting off circulation to the extremities and forcing more blood into the core. Hands and feet become starved of blood and cool rapidly. To lessen this effect, you need to keep as much of the body as possible covered to preserve body heat.

Physically the body will respond to heat loss by trying to generate heat by shivering. Shivering does help but it is not constant – nor is it the same in every case. Some people will shiver continually for long periods, while others will shiver in short bursts. Nevertheless the result is the same; shivering uses muscles, muscles need blood to operate and blood brings warmth. Obviously, when we use muscles we increase the need for the body to produce energy; this can only be successful if you have enough food to turn into energy.

7. Surviving in Wet Conditions

There are two types of cold conditions: cold dry, and cold wet. Cold dry is bad enough, but when you add water the survival encounter becomes a whole lot worse.

When the body and clothing are wet, heat loss happens much more quickly, and consequently the body has to work a lot harder to keep up with this loss. You can become wet from three sources: direct water from rain or other water courses; indirect from snow and ice as it melts; and from the body's sweat. Having to work physically hard to survive in cold regions while trying to keep warm often means that you have to work fully clothed. The sweat permeates the clothing and the body heat melts snow and ice; the result is a lot of water held in your clothing, thus reducing its ability to insulate you effectively. Whenever possible, strip or add layers of clothing to regulate your body heat while working. If you have the luxury of a change of warm, dry clothing, keep these in your shelter to change into when you rest. If not, you should aim to dry your clothing at every opportunity – obviously, a fire is the ideal drying medium, but you may not be in a position to make one. In some cold areas it is possible to hang your clothing outside, allowing it to freeze and then knocking the ice crystals off by beating it with a stick or something similar. This crude freeze-dry method will not fully dry your clothes, but if carried out regularly it will get rid of excessive water.

One of the things you will have to get used to in cold wet conditions is damp clothing. Depending on your shelter, heating, the prevailing weather and the air temperature, you may have to put your spare clothing on top of your wet clothes. There have been many debates in survival-training circles about the merits of this action. In the survival situation the priority is to keep as warm as possible to prevent hypothermia (cooling of the body which reduces the level of oxygen supply to the vital organs), exposure (severe chilling of the body surface causing a progressive fall in body temperature) and exhaustion (a physical condition adding to the deficiency of body heat); see the section on *First Aid* for further information. You can only do this by reducing heat loss, which is best achieved by adding clothing, giving you a better chance of trapping body heat between the layers. The clothing should not be tight, otherwise it will restrict circulation.

Wherever possible, keep out of the rain and snow. Putting a layer of insulation – such as spruce boughs or some other thick padding – between you and the ground will reduce the thawing that takes place when the body comes into contact with snow and ice.

When it is constantly wet from sweat, rain and melt water the skin becomes saturated. In this state it is very prone to injury, and sores soon break out – if not properly dealt with, they will become infected. All footwear also loses its protective properties when subjected to long exposure to water and ice. Blisters on the heels and toes often go unnoticed owing to the numbing effect of the cold and wet, while frostbite takes hold very quickly and needs to be prevented at all costs.

Body heat is further reduced when wind is added; the wind blows the body heat away and rapidly chills the skin. This is especially dangerous in conjunction with wet conditions.

In the survival situation it is important to understand the relationship between wind chill (the cooling power on the body in relation to the wind speed), the cold and the wet. These three components together account for many deaths and should not be underestimated.

When considering your protection, you should first establish the prevailing wind direction. At first you may consider that the wind direction you are encountering at the time is the prevailing direction, and clearly you will need to act accordingly to shelter from it there and then. The initial shelter may not be in the best position for your permanent dwelling, and may well expose you to the long-term danger from constant winds because you have positioned the mouth of your shelter into the prevailing wind. You can use local signs to work out the usual direction – for example, trees will grow bending away from the prevailing wind, and a row of tall bushes will show stunted growth on the side from which the wind usually blows.

Wind is defined in two ways: the direction from which it blows, and the speed. Both are important to the survivor, but the speed is the most important factor, as this will have an effect on wind chill. In 1883, a British naval hydrographer, Admiral Sir Francis Beaufort, devised a scale of wind speed that was adopted by the Admiralty in 1883 and is now internationally recognized as the Beaufort Scale.

The mean air temperature in your location may be well above the level of danger from freezing to death. But the wind speed can cause the wind chill to lower your body temperature to a critical point.

THE BEAUFORT SCALE

Wind Speed (mph)	Scale	Force	Description
1	0	Calm	Smoke rises vertically
1 - 3	1	Light air	Wind direction shown by smoke
4 - 7	2	Slight breeze	Wind felt on face, leaves rustle
8 - 12	3	Gentle breeze	Leaves, twigs in constant motion
13 - 18	4	Moderate breeze	Raises dust, small branches moved, snow drifts
19 - 24	5	Fresh breeze	Small trees sway, wavelets form on inland water
25 - 31	6	Strong breeze	Large branches in motion, high drifting snow
32 - 38	7	High wind	Whole trees in motion, difficult walking, visibility obscured by drifting snow
39 - 46	8	Gale	Twigs break, slow progress when walking
46 - 54	9	Strong gale	Branches break
55 - 63	10	Whole gale	Trees uprooted
64 - 72	11	Storm	Widespread damage
73 - 83	12	Hurricane	Hurricane

Being able to determine wind speed is an essential skill in reducing the risk of wind chill and storm damage.

8. Surviving in Hot Conditions

It goes without saying that the main problem for the survivor is the sun and its associated heat. The sun is an extremely dangerous force that is often overlooked until the damage is done – it is far easier to shield the effects of the sun's rays than it is to attend to the damage it does.

Always keep as much of your body as possible covered with thin loose layers of clothing. Not only will they protect you from the sun's rays, but they will also trap sand and dust, and allow cooler air to pass through to the skin.

The constant glare of the sun can damage the eyes. If you have sunglasses or goggles, keep them on. If not, make a pair of shades by cutting card, material, bark, or some other medium shaped to fit and with two thin slits to cut down on the glare.

In sand deserts, wear a face cloth to protect you from the wind-blown sand. Quite often you will be subjected to a sandstorm or a whirlwind known as a *sand devil* that will whip up and engulf you in sand and dust. At these times, keep your eyes and mouth closed, and use a cloth to filter out the particles as you breathe through your nose.

Meanwhile, avoid walking or resting in dried riverbeds, as these *wadis* can flood without warning.

Salt loss

In hot climates, you can expect to sweat a great deal. Sweating is the body's way of dealing with heat, and its function is to help to reduce the inner body heat from becoming too high. The majority of people know that they can die very quickly from the cold, but many people do not realize that heat can also kill.

As we sweat, we obviously lose body fluids; therefore keeping the body replenished with sufficient fluid to sustain this loss is one of the most important aspects of survival (see the section on *Water*). What is not so obvious is the loss of essential minerals including salt, which is carried out of the body by sweat; the act of drinking water alone will not address this deficiency. Evaporating water from the sea is one way of obtaining salt, although this is not a very efficient way of maintaining the loss from the body as sea-water only contains around 3% of salt; it would take a lot of processing for little reward. The best way to replenish lost salt is to eat foods such as locally caught game and fish, and a number of plants also carry a relatively high level of salt (see the section on *Food*). Unfortunately, being in hot climates tends to lessen your appetite, but you must fight against this tendency and continue to eat normally. Reducing sweating by working and moving in the cooler parts of the day and night is the most effective way of reducing the risk of body fluid loss.

Heat very quickly saps energy and makes personal motivation very difficult. It is sometimes extremely hard to carry out even the simplest of tasks to support the survival effort. The lack of proper diet, water and the stress of the survival situation will drag morale down, and the much-needed psychology of the will to survive will be tested to its limits.

Along with the mind, the human body is taken to its extremes. In hot deserts, sand and dust cling to the sweating body, causing sores and blisters which need to be dealt with as soon as they appear (see *Long-term Medical Problems*). In the tropics the constant wet conditions make the skin frail; it can easily break open, and wounds will quickly become infected and often infested with an incredible number of parasites. Keeping as cool and as clean as possible will help you to survive in these very testing conditions.

Many people have survived in hot conditions, even with the most appalling injuries. If they can, so can you!

9. Surviving Water

Much of the Earth's surface is covered in sea water. Add to this the millions of rivers and lakes, and you will realize that the chances are that your survival encounter is probably going to mean that you will either have to navigate vast expanses of water, or at the very least that you will be faced with having to negotiate a river.

As a hazard, water creates a very hostile and harsh environment. On open water there is no hiding place from the weather – there is nowhere to go to keep out of the wind or the sun. Water is never still: it is constantly moving and always dangerous. The strength of movement and the depth is determined by the weather – especially the wind and rain – as well as the water's currents caused by its flow. Being able to read water is an important survival skill. Before you decide to negotiate flowing waters, take the time to properly assess the best position at which to cross. On large, open water, be aware of the effect the wind will have on you and any craft you may decide to construct or use as a means for your escape.

Many people have survived by constructing a raft or a sailing dinghy. Generally speaking, you are more likely to have been put into a survival situation because of a mishap such as a shipwreck, or because of an accident involving some form of floating craft such as a small boat capsizing or an inflatable being blown away from a holiday beach. In any event, being able to right a capsized boat is one of the fundamental skills in water survival.

There are a number of ways in which you can be subjected to a capsized or inverted boat. It may be due to a large wave, strong winds, inexperience or simply the craft having been inappropriately launched. The cause doesn't really matter; the fact is that you will be exposed and floating around in a hostile environment.

If a capsize does happen, the first thing to remember is not to lose contact with your craft. Keep hold of it and hang on until you can re-organize yourself. The shock of being launched into the cold water will take your breath away, and you need to act quickly to maintain your composure. If you are using sails as a means of propulsion, you must manoeuvre the boat so that your back is to the prevailing wind, with your boat and its sails in front of you. If there are two or more of you, then one of the others needs to be at the front of the boat and in a position to be scooped up when the boat is righted. The rest of the group should be in touch with the boat and help in righting it. One person should then climb onto the daggerboard of the craft (keep as close as possible to the hull of the boat to avoid putting too much pressure on the daggerboard and breaking it). If there is no daggerboard to use as a lever, grab hold at the rail where the hull meets the side deck and place your feet on the hull, leaning back to use your weight to right the boat – it will leave the water slowly at first, but once the sail clears the water the process becomes much easier.

RIGHTING A DINGHY

Being able to right a boat in an emergency is a simple technique that can be easily carried out.

If you have been a passenger in an aircraft that has had to ditch in the sea, then you will probably be in the position of having to use one of the inflatable dinghies stowed for this eventuality. You should also be wearing a regulation buoyancy aid incorporating a light and an inflation tube. Once you are aboard the dinghy, you should steer it away from the aircraft to a safe distance in case it explodes or quickly sinks and causes you to be sucked under with it. Attend to any damage to the dinghy as soon as possible (there is usually a repair kit stowed in an inner pocket). Once you are clear, attend to any first-aid requirements that you or anyone else have. Where possible, protect against the cold, either by putting extra clothes on or sharing body heat (see *Surviving Cold Conditions*). If there are other survival craft in the area, join up with them and tie all the floating craft together. As soon as possible, prepare your signalling equipment and make it ready for use. Stores and food may well be floating around the crash site; you should collect as much of this as possible without putting yourself or others in danger.

Protection from the weather should be your next consideration. It may be that you have a dinghy that has a hood; if so, this should be tightly fastened, but if not, try to construct a shield from spare clothing or anything else to hand. There may be fresh water already placed in the craft, or it may be fitted with a solar still system; where there isn't one, you may have to construct a fresh-water collection system using watertight material to catch any rainwater. It may even be necessary to ration water to start with until you can properly assess the situation. There may be a store of food that also needs rationing, or you may have to rely on food you have to catch (see the section on *Food*). If there are any survival pamphlets aboard the craft, take the time to read them and act on the advice given. Finally, make a plan of action including a shift pattern to ensure that there is always one person ready to use the signals and another to steer and sail the craft.

Inflatable craft are usually light, and can be badly launched and inverted or end up in this position because of waves or high winds. If this is the case, swim around the craft as soon as possible so that the wind is blowing in your face. Once in position, use your weight to push down on the craft so that it leaves the water. Once the wind can get under it, it will be flipped over: remember to keep hold of it throughout this manoeuvre. Once the craft is the right way up, swim around so that the wind is blowing from behind you, and board the craft. As soon as you are safely aboard, bale out any water inside and follow the procedures outlined above.

RIGHTING AN INFLATABLE

Inverted boats, canoes and dinghies have an air pocket that allows you to breathe until you can swim clear. Lifting a corner of an inflatable so the wind can get under it will help you to right the craft.

The tides, wind and currents are the tools of navigation on large areas of open water. Tides rise and then fall approximately every 12 hours, and the sun and the moon's gravitational pull control these highs and lows. Their greatest strength is when the earth, sun and moon are in line, which happens every 14 days or so. The tides can be very high at this time, and are known as spring tides, whereas when the earth, sun and moon are out of line the pull is less and consequently the tides are relatively low. It takes approximately six hours for a high tide to change to a low tide, and the pull is much stronger around the three- to four-hour points (it is when the tide is going out that most people are swept away to sea). Understanding the relationship between the tides, wind and currents can help you to steer your craft. Clearly, if you have a sail that you can adjust, then the wind will often be the most important aid to the boat's propulsion and navigation. However, if the sail is fixed or you have no sail at all, then your ability to steer the craft is restricted. For example, you might be able to see land, but the wind could be blowing you away from it or the current is pulling you away. Keeping a watch on the tides, currents and wind may help you to set a course. In essence, if you stay very low in the craft and keep any sails down and collapse your shelter or cover, the wind is less likely to determine your course; the currents and tides will have the advantage. So if you are in sight of land and the wind is blowing you off course, you can lower the craft's wind resistance and use the currents and inbound tide to pull you in and make a landfall. Or if the wind can assist you, construct a sail or sit high in the craft to catch the wind and use it to push you in.

Being able to swim is an obvious survival skill. If you are forced to swim for safety, leave your clothing on and swim very slowly to conserve energy; the swim will be much easier if you have some form of buoyancy aid. If you cannot see land or you do not swim well, stay with any wreckage and hang on until help arrives.

If you see someone in the water and they are in trouble, summon help before you do anything else. Wherever possible, stay out of the water yourself and effect a rescue by throwing a line, using a long pole for the swimmer to hold onto or make a human chain. If you are a very strong swimmer and have decided to effect a rescue from the water, do not dive into the water, but enter it slowly. Keep away from the victim and use clothing or a short line for them to hold onto so that you can haul them to safety. If you have no alternative but to grab the person, approach them from behind and talk to them all the time to calm them down; a frightened drowning person will cling onto you so tightly that they are likely to hamper your swimming and drown you with them.

Fast-flowing water such as rivers and floods should not be negotiated unless there really is no alternative. If they have to be crossed and you can afford the time, wait until the levels drop. Unfortunately, in the survival situation, time is often of the essence and you may well have to cross. Trying to hop from boulder to boulder in an effort to keep your feet dry will end in disaster; wet rocks are slippery, and fallen trees have a habit of moving and rolling if they are stood on – all this adds up to an accident waiting to happen. If the water is shallow enough to wade into, wear your footwear – taking your socks off is acceptable. When crossing, choose a spot where the current or flow is mild, and try to keep away from submerged trees and other hazards. Cross steadily using one of the methods described below. Do not balance on submerged rocks: feel the river bed with your feet until you can fully place your foot down flat. Do not over-stretch, as you can be unbalanced very easily by even the mildest of currents. Once you are in the water, continually look upstream, keeping your wits about you and watching for debris that is being swept along and may be a hazard to you. Move slightly towards the flow on a diagonal course. If you are carrying a pack, release it and carry it by one strap over the downstream arm; be ready to let it go if you get into trouble, as holding onto it will pull you under the water. The body should be angled to lessen the resistance. Move one leg first and then bring the other to it – crossing the legs will lead to a loss of balance. A stout staff placed upstream can be used as a third leg, and also used as a probe and a depth gauge. Attach as many flotation aids as possible to the arms – empty containers and air-filled plastic bags are ideal.

A group can safely cross by way of a rope circle. The strongest member is attached to the continual loop and crosses in the manner described above; one person holds the rope upstream another downstream. Once across, a complete circle is formed that can be used as a safety line to get members across one by one. The last member crosses in the same way as the first. If anyone stumbles, the two anchormen guide him or her; these anchormen should move downstream with the fallen person, as standing fast and trying to stop or haul in the fallen person will result in his being forced below the waterline – he will naturally be guided into the bank if the anchormen move at the same rate as the flow of water.

If you don't have the luxury of a rope, you can move a group in steady flowing water that is not too deep by interlocking the arms, forming a circle and moving slowly together – each member watching out for the others. In faster-flowing water, it may well be safer to line up one behind the other in small groups, firmly holding the person in front and moving in the same way as the lone crosser described above. It is better if the two strongest members take the front and rear positions.

RIVER CROSSING

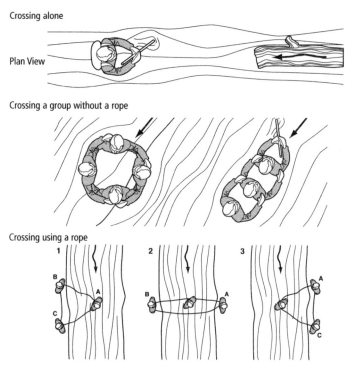

Crossing alone

Plan View

Crossing a group without a rope

Crossing using a rope

Unless it is absolutely necessary, avoid crossing any water hazards. If you do have to cross, take the time to plan your route across properly.

If you are caught up in floods, make every effort to move to high ground. And if you are caught out, it is better to go onto the rooves of sturdy buildings than to climb to the tops of trees, because if the soil becomes waterlogged and unstable it is often washed away, exposing the tree's roots and weakening its anchorage. If the tree is washed away, there is a real danger that you will be tangled in its branches and unable to break free. If you have no alternative but to take refuge in a tree, then be ready to vacate it in an emergency.

Whether you have been forced to leave your tree, high ground, rooftop or have simply been swept away, you must turn yourself into a sitting position with your legs pointing downstream. As the current takes you, keep looking forward and using your arms to steer as safe a course as possible. By keeping your feet high in front of you, you will be in a position to take the impact of any boulders that you may be forced into. By looking ahead you can also read the water; for example, a sudden swell appearing (especially with a back eddy) indicates a hidden danger just below the surface, while an outcrop of rock can have a relatively calm area of water behind it. If you are caught up in an eddy or in the water directly below a weir or waterfall feature, you can escape by diving down below it and using the water's natural force to project you out of the hazard.

SWEPT AWAY

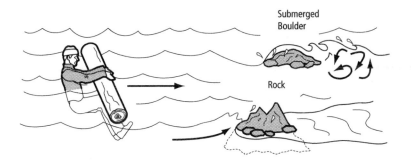

If you have to swim or are swept away, pick a spot on a downstream bank or high ground some distance away and slowly ferry glide across. Use clothing etc. to spread your weight when negotiating swaps and waterlogged ground.

Whenever you are faced with water hazards that you can anticipate, take the time to construct or find floating aids. These can simply be floating timber, or you can use trousers tied at the bottoms, filled with fresh air and held tight at the top – normal clothing used in this way will hold the air better if it is wet first. Waterproof clothing is also windproof, and consequently once it is filled with air it keeps afloat for much longer.

If you are adrift for long periods in calm waters such as lakes and seas, you can conserve your heat and energy by carrying out drown-proofing procedures. This is done by taking a normal breath, relaxing and adopting a crouching position and allowing the body to float just below the surface.

Stay in this position for as long as you can comfortably, then push down with your arms to force you back to the surface, lift your head out of the water and take a breath of air, and adopt the crouch position again.

Once you approach land, you may well have to negotiate an area of mud or swamp. You can swim over this type of ground without sinking if you use your clothing spread out in front of you, and place your arms, head and chest on top and carry out very wide, slow breaststroke actions – recovering your clothing as you pass over it and spreading it out in front of you again until you reach solid land.

There are times when you may come across an area of swamp. Quite often you can determine these areas by the plant life they support – tough grasses growing in tussocks, bright green vegetation and reeds are good indicators of waterlogged land. Moving through swamps and bogs is extremely hard work and very slow-going. If you do find yourself in this type of terrain and you start to sink, do not panic. Lying down and spreading your body out will slow down the sinking action long enough for a colleague to help you or for you to breaststroke out to safety. Avoid thrashing around, as this will cause you to sink quickly.

Escape from a sunken vehicle

If you are driving, do not attempt to cross swollen rivers or flooded areas. A number of deaths occur each year as a result of people trying to drive through floods. Firstly, they rarely know the true depth of the water and, secondly, they drive across the current without realizing its force; before they know it, the car is being swept away and soon turns over.

If you are unfortunate enough to be in a vehicle that has entered deep water, then you should act quickly to get clear of the vehicle before it sinks. If you do not have the time to evacuate, keep the windows fully closed and release your seat-belt. In deep water the vehicle will sink because it will be dragged down by the heavy engine – unless there is a heavy load in the boot, of course. If the heaviest end is the front, then you have the opportunity to move into the back seats and exit from the back doors; this has to be carried out during the first seconds of the vehicle sinking. Once the vehicle completely sinks and finally comes to rest, the chances are that you will be completely disorientated, but do not panic (easier said than done, I know). With the doors and windows shut, the vehicle will not be filled with water straight away, so use the time wisely: there is air in the vehicle, even if it seems as though there isn't any. Water will filter in from the bottom up and it will normally be so dirty that you will not be able to see very well. Because of the pressure of water from the outside, opening the doors will be impossible at first. When you are ready to evacuate, open a window slowly, controlling the inflow of water. As you do this, the pressure between the inside and outside will begin to equalize. At the last moment, take a normal breath of air and fully open the window so that the water completely fills the vehicle. As it does this, watch the direction of the air bubbles: they will be heading for the surface, and you need to follow them to safety. With the vehicle full of water, you should be able to open the doors to escape, but if you can't, get out through the window. In any event, when you leave, come out head first facing the vehicle all the way as though you are performing a forward roll. The reason for this is that you can bend virtually double from the stomach, whereas your back movement is very restricted and may cause you to become stuck against the wreckage if you try to come out backwards.

10. Surviving Fire

The problem with fire is that it can spread at an alarming rate – especially when it has enough fuel and oxygen to keep it going. The way to put out a fire is to restrict the fuel and starve it of oxygen. In the majority of cases, if you are caught up in a fire you should get as far away from it as possible without delay. Unless it is a very small fire or you have the experience and equipment to extinguish it, leave it alone and get out of its way. In some situations, of course, you may not be able to get out easily, in which case you will have to assess the best way of dealing with the situation.

If you own a vehicle, then you should ensure that it is equipped with a fire extinguisher ready to be used in an emergency. Likewise you should make sure that you have extinguishers positioned around your home and workplace. Be aware that not all extinguishers are the same; some cannot be used on certain types of fire – for example, a water-based extinguisher becomes dangerous if you use it on an electrical fire. Always check the extinguishers you acquire to make sure what kind of fires they can be used on and how they are actually operated; also let other people around you know the way to use them in an emergency. Most extinguishers have a limited shelf-life, so they should be checked regularly.

Fire extinguisher tips

- Fires that are fuelled by paper, wood and textiles can be extinguished using powder, water or spray-foam extinguishers
- Vehicle fires should be extinguished using spray foam or powder-filled extinguishers only
- Spray foam, CO_2 gas and powder should be used on flammable liquids: do not use water
- Gas-fuelled fires should only be extinguished using CO_2 or powder extinguishers
- Where electricity is present, use only CO_2 or powder; if possible, you should also disconnect the electricity supply.

If you are visiting a building that you are expecting to stay in for some time – especially if you intend to sleep there – make sure that you can locate the extinguishers easily, and that you have checked the way they work. Be absolutely sure about this, as the next time you have to find and operate them may well be in an emergency and in the dark. Wherever you are staying, make sure that you know the best and quickest route to safety. If there are signed emergency exits, walk them and make sure that they are clear of obstructions. If you are not satisfied with them, tell those in charge to attend to the problem or ask for a move to another room where the exit is better. If you are still not happy or there is no chance of you being moved, take the time to look around the building and work out an alternative route to safety. Make sure that you know how doors and windows open, and check that they are not locked.

When properly fitted and regularly maintained, smoke alarms are one of the most effective warnings of fire, and save lives every day. If you do not have them fitted in your house, office, caravan, boat or whatever, then attend to this without delay. Once again, if you find yourself in an area where smoke alarms are fitted, check that they are working properly; if this proves difficult, ask to see the maintenance schedule. Do not accept that they are working simply because they are fitted.

If a fire breaks out in your car, it will normally be in the engine compartment, although this is not by any means the only place in which the fire can break out. Electrical fires can start behind the dashboard –usually indicated by a strong smell of melting wiring sleeves. If you can smell burning at all, pull over and check the vehicle thoroughly. If you can see smoke billowing out from under the bonnet, do not open it – by opening it, you allow more oxygen in, and the flames will leap out and could seriously burn you or set light to your clothing. Once you have established that a fire is present, move away from the vehicle and alert the emergency services: do not go back into the vehicle to retrieve anything you have left behind, as the fire can spread to the fuel pipes and tank, blowing up the vehicle without warning.

Aircraft can develop a fire due to impact, a short in the wiring or an engine fault. If there is an engine fire, the pilots will be in a position to deal with this effectively, as the majority of aeroplane engines are fitted with a fire-extinguisher system that is operated from the flight-deck. Inside, cabin crew are trained to deal with fire, and the plane will land as soon as possible. When fire does take hold, the cabin can fill with dense, black smoke, but if you drop down to the floor you will be able to get some air. Once you are down, stay there and look for the illuminated strips that are either placed on the floor or on the base of the seats and which indicate the way to the nearest exit, and follow them to safety.

I used to work in an area where the fire-bombing of buildings was a problem. As a result, I was given training from the UK's fire service to learn how to safely evacuate a building that was on fire. A part of that training consisted of moving through a series of smoke-filled rooms and negotiating obstacles. If you stood up, you were completely blinded by the dense smoke, but when lying flat on the floor the smoke was not as dense; from the lower position, I could see well enough to crawl to safety. even in these controlled surroundings I felt extremely vulnerable.

As with all aspects of survival, panic and fear lead to poor decision-making and ultimately death. If you are confronted with fire and smoke in a confined space, keep calm and logically work a way out of the situation.

If you find yourself in a room with smoke filtering in through the cracks around the door, do not open it. Put the back of your hand close to the door panels: if the fire is directly outside, you will feel the heat; if you cannot feel any heat, carefully touch the door with the back of your hand – but be ready to pull it away quickly to lessen any burn injury. If it is cool to the touch, carefully open the door and follow your emergency exit route. If it is hot, assume the fire is outside and keep the door closed, using wet bedding or any other material to plug the gap under the door, then move to a window and either escape or attract attention to yourself.

If you can safely leave the room but are stopped from getting out of the building because of the fire, move to a room as far away from the seat of the fire as possible. Avoid going higher in the building. If it is possible to jump without injury, or you have a rope or enough bedding or other material to manufacture one, use the abseil technique explained in the *Search-and-Rescue* section, or use the building-escape technique explained in the *Hostage* section. If you do evacuate in either of these ways, it will be safer if you choose an area to land on where the ground is soft, or you may be able to cushion your landing area by first throwing out bedding and other soft furnishings.

SMOKE FILLED ROOM

Before opening any doors, carefully feel the door – if it is hot, assume the fire is on the other side: do not open the door!

Fires in the open are usually easier to escape from, but you must react positively to effect your escape. One of the deciding factors is the wind; basically, whichever way the wind is blowing determines the direction the fire takes and the speed of its advance. If you are in a forest and you are not sure which way to go, the wildlife will be moving away from the fire, and this will give you an idea of the best direction to follow. In managed woodland, foresters leave wide paths called firebreaks between trees so that if a fire does start it will be starved of fuel when it reaches these areas and halted. If you are completely cut off and can find a pool of water or a stream, lie down in it using a hollow reed or carved wooden tube as a breathing pipe and submerge yourself in the water. If there is a fast-flowing river you may be forced to jump into it and use its flow to float you out of harm's way. Using rivers in this way is obviously dangerous, and only you can make the decision to go to this extreme (see section on *Surviving Water*).

11. Street Survival

No matter where we are in the world, be it in a small town or the streets of a major city, street crime happens. There are many reasons why people resort to crime, but the more important question for the survivor is: how do they choose their victims in the first place? Is it just a case of being in the wrong place at the wrong time? If it is as simple as that – and the evidence points exactly to this explanation – then what we have to do to survive is to be in the right place at the right time. What this actually means is taking precautions to avoid becoming a victim by reducing our profile as a potential target, and actively thinking about crimes against the person, how to avoid them and our day-to-day survival. For the most part, the majority of people feel safe and comfortable in their local environment – there is still a risk of your become a victim of crime but you lessen it by using your knowledge of the environment and the types of people living around you. As a result, you know not to go to certain places or to associate with particular unsavoury people; the problem often comes when you move away from the places and people you know.

No army would go into battle without knowing the type of location in which they were to be deployed; a boxer would not take on an opponent without knowing how big they were or their style of boxing. Yet many of us travel around the world often without any background knowledge of the cities, towns and villages we are going to visit. Before embarking on any trip – no matter how small – you should always take time to learn something about the place and its people. If there are particularly dangerous areas, you need to know this so that you can avoid going to them, or if you have no alternative you can at least ascertain the safest time to travel or how to arrange an escort.

Where there are people, trouble is not far behind. Theft is the second oldest profession in the world: if you walk around with a bag of money on show, someone will go for it! Unless they are very desperate, the chances are that they will wait until you are in a lonely, isolated place, or at a location where they know they can easily escape after committing the crime.

You can reduce the risk of becoming a target by keeping away from the places that you know are potential trouble-spots. If there is an area that is known as a dangerous neighbourhood, keep away from it, and if you aren't sure where these places are, ask the local police, the tourist information centre or the owners of the hotel in which you are staying. When you are out and about, think as the criminal does – he is less likely to strike if you are walking down a busy, well-lit street, whereas if you go into the back streets where there are fewer people and the lighting is poor, you will increase your profile as a potential target. When you can, cross intersections on the surface and avoid using underpasses – especially isolated ones or those that are poorly lit. If there is no alternative, wait until you can walk through with a group of people. If you are attending business meetings or going to a friend's apartment, try to make the appointments early in the day to avoid having to leave the premises late; this is especially important if the places you are visiting are isolated office blocks or industrial units, or are located out of town. The car parks and local areas may have many vehicles parked in them and be very busy when you arrive, but after normal working hours the chances are that the vehicles have gone and the whole area becomes quiet, dark and threatening.

There are four main factors that incite theft and violence. The first is money, or the lack of it. The second factor is pure hatred – racial, religious, political, or whatever. It doesn't really matter what the reasoning is; if your face does not fit, someone will want to punch it. The third factor is best described as tribal; it is similar to the second, but its roots are communal, perhaps relating to belonging to a gang or groups of rival soccer supporters. These groups generally prey on similar, like-minded groups and organizations. The problem is that once they begin their crimes of violence, innocent people become involved. The fourth reason for crime against the person is sexual – rape is the obvious one, but others include sexual assaults and sexual abuse against children.

Having worked in the investigation and prevention of sexual abuse against children, I can tell you that the perpetrators of these crimes are extremely quick to recognize a target child, and even quicker at acting on that recognition to draw an unsuspecting, innocent child into their clutches – even when their parents are close by.

In all four of the above motives the criminal looks for the opportunity. Quite often the best opportunities are found when the targets are out of their usual environment and clubbed together – as is the case when people go on holiday. All the components are there: the relaxed atmosphere putting them off their guard, luggage, money, children, late-night drinking and dancing. It is in the resorts and on the usual routes to them that the majority of organized street crime takes place. Even the accommodation gives no real protection – in many resorts around the world, criminals are closely linked to the hotel and guesthouse managers and owners: a second set of door and hire-car keys is given to the criminals in return for a share of the money.

In bars and discos, criminals watch and wait for the right target – usually some unsuspecting happy-hour reveller who has been flashing their money around without realizing the implications and are clearly the worse for drink, or who have had their drinks spiked with drugs to make sure that they are not going to be capable of protecting themselves when the crime takes place.

To protect against becoming a target, the best policy is to visit clubs, bars and discos that are members-only and are situated in the main city streets. Some clubs state that they are members-only, but in fact allow anyone in on the night, taking extra money off them as a joining fee. Be in control of your drinking, and watch for any unusual actions of the bar staff. Be aware of your surroundings and the people you are mixing with – if you feel uncomfortable or uneasy, trust your feelings and leave early, or make sure you have a taxicab waiting for you.

When you are out and about, if you suspect that someone is following you, quicken your pace a little. If you do not put any distance between them and you, it may indicate that they have quickened their pace to keep up with you. If the street is shop-lined and busy, go into one of the shops and wait for the person to go by: you cannot be followed from the front so, as long as you keep the person in front of you, you are in control. However, do make sure that they have not got an accomplice who has taken up following you from the rear. If you still feel that you are being followed, ask a shopkeeper or passer-by the way to the local police station; it may be very close, in which case you can walk there quickly. If you are still not sure, try crossing the street; if the person also crosses over, then you have to assume that your suspicions are founded – in which case you have to ask for help there and then. Do not expose yourself to more danger by walking off the main streets, walking into a dead-end or trying to take a short-cut over fields or derelict areas.

Before you embark on a journey in an area with which you are not familiar, make sure you know the exact route to take: there really is no excuse for poor preparation. Most towns and cities have decent A to Z street atlases. Buy one and study it; look out for prominent features and important buildings such as the local police station and hospital; ask the hotel staff or someone you can trust to mark the maps and indicate the high crime areas and other places where you should not go. If there are no maps, ask for the best route to take or use a proper taxicab.

Think about the most sensible clothing to wear. Tiny skirts and low blouses for women should be avoided, as these may be provocative, while if you wear tight trousers your wallet can easily be located. Shorts may not have enough pockets to carry your valuables in, forcing you to walk around carrying your cash and credit cards in your hand. Even when you do not feel confident, look as if you are. One of the triggers criminals use to locate a suitable target is behaviour that shows a person to be unsure, or lost. Make sure that you are alert, and always stand and act as though you are totally in control of yourself and your surroundings. Do not fumble about with your money, and if you are using currency you are not familiar with, keep low-denomination notes in one pocket, medium-denomination in another and high-value notes in another. By doing this you will avoid having to peel off several high-value notes to get to the lower denominations in full view of everyone around you. Take your time in paying, and do not get flustered.

If you have to go to a cash machine or local bank, carry out your transaction keeping very close to the machine or counter to stop anyone from seeing your personal identification number or the amount of cash you have withdrawn.

Tips to avoid being targeted for street crime

- Walk and act with absolute confidence – even when you're lost, act as though you belong where you are
- Keep your camera, shopping bags and handbags close to and in front of your body; if you carry a bag with a strap, wear it with the strap across your body
- Walk facing the oncoming traffic; by doing this, you will avoid the risk

of a car pulling up behind you and someone snatching your luggage
- Keep to the centre of the walkway; avoid walking close to doorways and entrances, as it is in these areas that criminals often lurk
- Do not drink so much alcohol that you are not in control
- Keep to well-lit streets and main highways
- Wear clothing that is practical and not provocative; loose clothing with plenty of pockets allows you to carry your money, credit cards, passport and so on without signalling the fact
- Keep away from known trouble-spots
- Avoid gangs of youngsters
- Make sure that you know the political, religious and racial feeling of the areas you are travelling through or visiting
- Keep well away from derelict buildings, large areas of open deserted land, shrub-filled parkland and isolated office and industrial units
- Stay with the majority of the local people; avoid becoming isolated and alone
- Do not stop if asked for directions; keep walking as if you haven't heard
- Use properly licensed taxicabs and other transport
- Carry a personal attack alarm, a torch and a whistle
- If you think you are being followed, assume you are and make your way directly to a police station, call for assistance or seek refuge in a local shop or private dwelling.

12. Self-Defence/Defending Others

The best form of self-defence and survival is to avoid getting into a physically violent situation in the first place. When you feel that you may be subjected to one, move away from the aggressor if possible. If this is impracticable, try to negotiate your way out of trouble. Never underestimate the power of speech: if you can reason with the aggressor and turn them away from a physically violent act, then you have achieved the ultimate goal – stopping yourself or others being injured or killed (see *Surviving People, Effective Communication* and *Developing Awareness*).

If you can see that a particular area is unsafe or that a group of people have violent tendencies or are carrying weapons, do not get involved with them. Whenever you are travelling – especially in unfamiliar territory – be on the lookout for possible escape routes and places of safety.

It is a fact of life that people will and do resort to physical violence. The problem is that you cannot always tell who is dangerous and who is not. Because someone is tall and broad with tattoos and earrings, it does not mean that you should be wary of them. Be wary of everyone you do not know well, and expect the unexpected. Reducing the risk of you becoming a target is the first part of your self-defence (see *Surviving People*).

However, when there is no alternative, and you are faced with a violent confrontation against you or someone you care for or have responsibility for, then you have to fight back. Your fight should be very aggressive, and you should aim to stop the aggressor completely by physically beating him. Although you may not be a naturally aggressive person or a fighter, there is no reason why you cannot overpower a much heavier, more experienced, violent person. If you start with the confidence to beat them, the aggressor will be surprised and may give up the fight there and then. Most bullies are cowards, and usually choose their targets on the basis that the person is weaker than they are and easily intimidated. Show them you are not a pushover, and you may create an advantage.

There are thousands of fighting and self-defence techniques. My particular favourite is Tae Kwon Do, but unless you practise very regularly, you will soon lose your edge. Because of this, I believe that it is better for non-fighters to concentrate on a small number of proven techniques that are easy to master and remember in time of crisis. If you already have preferred techniques, keep using them and develop them so that you can perform them effectively at any time. When you do practise fighting techniques, wear everyday clothing and footwear that you would be wearing when you are travelling. Learning fighting techniques wearing trainers, sportswear, boxing gloves and protective pads is not realistic, and you will be surprised how different the moves feel when you are restricted by your clothing or you do not have full grip with your footwear.

When an attack happens, do not expect the aggressor to tell you he is going to attack you. There is a millisecond between verbal aggression and physical attack. If you have not read the situation, the chances are that the attack will be launched when you are totally unprepared (see *Surviving People*).

Keeping your balance and being able to lessen any damage from an initial attack is very important. If you feel that an attack may happen, move into a position to defend yourself. This doesn't mean that you should jump into it at the start of verbal aggression. Moving into it without letting the aggressor know will put you on your guard, and you will be in a position to act if the confrontation escalates to violence. Of course, if you are assaulted without verbal indication, you should snap into a basic defence stance straight away. Remember, in all of this, as I stated earlier, it is permissible to use reasonable force to defend yourself and this force can extend to killing your aggressor, if they present a real threat to your life or the life of another. Excessive force, however, beyond what is justified by the facts of the situation, must not be used. As I have outlined above, the best policy is to avoid, if possible, violent situations but to be ready to defend yourself, and others, appropriately if there is no alternative.

BASIC DEFENCE STANCE

Be ready for an initial attack, and always look for an escape route. The description shows the stance for a right-handed person. If you are left-handed, simply start with the right shoulder and adjust the rest accordingly.

The basic defence stance

The stance that I prefer for people who are not used to fighting is the basic stance shown above. This can be adopted quickly in an immediate attack, or slowly moved into without letting your opponent know that you are preparing to counter his attack. Firstly turn your body so that your left shoulder points at the aggressor. Position your feet firmly on the ground, pointing your left foot at him, and slightly bend the left knee. Slide the right leg back with the foot at a right-angle to the lead foot using it as a stabilizer; keeping the knee locked, you will have a very solid stance. This initial position reduces the attacker's target area and you can quickly go into the full defence stance by lifting your lead shoulder and tucking your chin behind it, which will lower your head pointing your forehead at the attacker. Keeping your mouth shut will avoid a broken jaw if you are hit. Lift your right hand up to cover the exposed side of your face, and drop your left hand down to defend against a kick to the groin. Lean back so that your head is out of the aggressor's reach, and be ready to fend off the initial attack. From this position you can easily launch a counter-attack, or run away if you feel you can escape.

The body's weapon system

The head
When you are close up to your aggressor, use your head to take him off balance by pushing it into his face. This is particularly effective in disrupting the aggressor while you are performing other techniques such as disarming him. From a front position about a half a metre (18ins) from him, lunge forward, pushing off your back foot forcefully and flicking your head forward to hit him full in the face. This blow should be delivered with great force – aim to hit the bridge of the aggressor's nose to smash it with the bony part of your high forehead. Avoid bending backwards before powering forward, as this will give the aggressor a warning of your intention.

Teeth
If you are being held close, use your teeth to bite hard into any of the aggressor's flesh. Aim to bite right through so that your teeth meet – the pain is excruciating, and even the most hardened aggressor will let go of you, especially if you are biting through one or more of his fingers.

Clenched fist
A blow with the fist should be delivered with the fist tightly closed and the thumb outside the fingers; the wrist should be rigid and not bent. The ideal point of impact is with the first and second knuckles only, as this concentrates the force. Aim your blow well, making sure that you hit a vital spot. The eyes, nose, just under the cheekbone and lower jaw are the

best upper body areas to hit. Landing a powerful blow to the soft area just below the breastbone where the ribs come together will knock the wind out of the aggressor, while if you are low enough, a sharp powerful blow to the lower stomach or testicles will bring your aggressor down.

To get the optimum force behind your fist, keep your feet firmly planted on the ground and swing using the hips to force your upper body around, transferring the whole of the body's weight and power to the shoulders as they pivot around and power all the action down the arm to put the ultimate strength behind the punch.

THE BODY'S WEAPON SYSTEM

Head   Heel of hand   Fingers

Teeth   Fist   Edge of hand

Knee   Kick

Practise all the different techniques on a punch bag or fighting dummy. Do not leave this until you are confronted with violence, as you will not have the confidence to properly deliver the blows.

Edge of the hand

The hand should be rigid with the fingers tightly kept together and straight. The thumb should be extended at a right-angle to the hand. The point of impact is the fleshy area half-way between the joint of the little finger and the wrist. The technique is to deliver the blow from a bent arm forcing it with speed and body power – either in a chopping action or by swinging the hand horizontally, keeping the palm face down.

The blow is most effective if you aim to hit the aggressor in the soft area located at the base of the skull where the neck meets it; this will knock the aggressor out. A sharp, powerful blow across the carotid artery will result in a lack of blood to the brain in the first instance and massive bruising – both of which will render the aggressor unconscious. A slicing/swinging blow just under the Adam's apple with sufficient force to flatten the windpipe will kill the aggressor. If you are being held by your clothing, pull back so that the aggressor's arm is straightened and use a chopping blow onto his forearm: this will result in a fracture to his ulna or radius.

Heel of the hand

Make a claw shape with the fingers and pull them back, exposing the heel of your hand. From a very close position – around 15cm (6ins) – you should force the heel of your hand up to hit the aggressor under the chin with a sharp, powerful blow, throwing his head back. If you can, pull him towards the blow with your free hand by using the collar of his shirt. A knee to the groin will also force the aggressor to drop his chin towards the blow, giving it a lot more force. At the same time, use your fingers to poke into his eyes to temporarily blind him.

Finger jab

Using your first and second fingers, fully extend them and part them as if showing a victory sign. Forcefully thrust them into the aggressor's eyes. The blow should come from a short distance, be very quick and use enough power to blind the aggressor. You should aim to force the fingers straight through the eyeballs.

Knee

The knee should be forced upwards in a sharp, single movement, the other leg acting as a stabilizer. The most appropriate area in which to land the knee blow is in the groin. Any attempt to deliver a blow in that region will cause the aggressor's head to come down as he bends the middle of his body in an attempt to evade the blow. The knee can also be used to deliver a blow to the outside of the upper leg approximately half-way between the knee and the hip. A blow delivered here hits the leg nerves and effectively deadens the muscle action, causing severe pain. The aggressor will have difficulty in walking, giving you the opportunity to escape.

THE BODY'S VULNERABLE POINTS:
FRONT VIEW

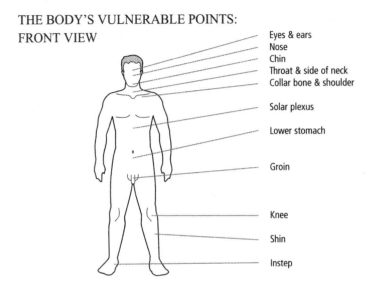

Eyes & ears
Nose
Chin
Throat & side of neck
Collar bone & shoulder

Solar plexus

Lower stomach

Groin

Knee

Shin

Instep

If you are attacked, counter with a strategic attack aiming for the most vulnerable points on the body.

REAR VIEW

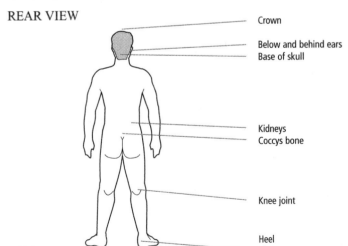

Crown

Below and behind ears
Base of skull

Kidneys
Coccys bone

Knee joint

Heel

You should attack the vulnerable points with your body's weapon system using the most appropriate blow for the job. If you have a weapon such as a heavy, short stick, make sure you deliver the blows in areas that will collapse the aggressor.

Kick

There are many ways of delivering an effective kick to an aggressor. However, without professional training the best way is to deliver the blow with the leg fully extended and the front of the shoe or boot used as the striking area. A kick allows you to be a good distance from the aggressor – if you are too close, then there is not enough force to do any real damage. The most effective distance is at the end of a fully stretched leg. Aim for the groin, but if the aggressor is on the floor, aim for his jaw, neck or throat.

The side and heel of the foot

A useful blow to use to good effect can be delivered if you are held very close to the aggressor, by using the side of your foot and your heel.

Lift your leg and place either the inside or outer edge of your foot just below the aggressor's knee, then stamp down, making sure the side of your foot scrapes down the shin and aiming the heel to come into contact with the bridge of his foot. As the heel hits, you should take your other foot off the ground to ensure that your full body weight powers your heel into the bridge of his foot. This often breaks the foot and collapses the bridge, so the aggressor is unable to pursue you if you decide to run away.

A killer blow can also be delivered to an aggressor who is lying on the floor either on his back or on his front. Jump in the air approximately half a metre (18ins) high, pull your toes back and the front of your foot upwards so that the first point of contact on landing is the edge of your heels, and land on the aggressor's lower chest or middle back. Landing in this way will concentrate all of your body weight and power in a small area, causing extensive damage and often sudden death to the aggressor.

Using a knife

Knives come in many sizes and styles. In essence, the most effective killing knife has a sharp point and two very sharp sides with a blade length of not less than 17cm (7ins). Carrying a knife in a public place without good reason or authority is a criminal offence. If an aggressor has pulled a knife on you, then it is likely that he is going to use it to kill or seriously injure you and you must prepare to respond appropriately.

I have been accidentally stabbed, taking the point of the blade in the underside of the little finger of my left hand. The point stuck into the bone at the middle finger joint. The pain was extreme and sent a cold shiver through the whole of my body; nevertheless once I had freed it from the bone, I could have continued fighting.

If you are faced by an attacker with a knife who is intent on killing you and youhave use of a knife to defend yourself, the following diagram shows the best knife attack areas. Knives kill by causing loss of blood; the greater the loss, the quicker the death. The body's main arteries are the most effective targets.

- Carotid: situated approximately 4cm (1.5ins) below the surface; severing it will cause unconsciousness within five seconds and death within 12 seconds.
- Subclavian: situated approximately 6cm (2ins) below the surface; severing it will cause unconsciousness within two seconds and death within four seconds.
- Heart: situated approximately 9cm (3ins) below the surface; severing it will cause unconsciousness within one second and death within three seconds.

KNIFE ATTACK POINTS

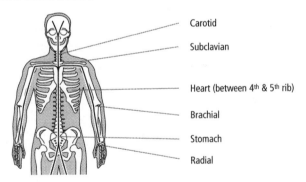

Carotid

Subclavian

Heart (between 4th & 5th rib)

Brachial

Stomach

Radial

Using a knife will bring an element of fear into the aggressor. Make sure that you keep a good hold on it so that it cannot be used against you.

- Brachial: situated approximately 2cm (1in) below the surface; severing it will cause unconsciousness within 14 seconds and death within two minutes.
- Radial: situated approximately 1cm (½in) below the surface; severing it will cause unconsciousness within 30 seconds and death within three minutes.

- Stomach: situated 12cm (5ins) below the surface; the length of time taken for the aggressor to become unconscious and die will be determined by the severity of the cut. If the stomach is the target chosen, a stabbing and cutting action should be used to cause the maximum amount of damage.

RELEASE TECHNIQUES

Speed is more essential than strength in these techniques. Once you have your opponent on the ground, you can deliver a killer blow by jumping in the air about a half a metre above the aggressor's body and landing with all your weight on your heels forcing them deep into his lower chest, neck or the middle of his back. With shoes on, this force is enough to cause serious damage and even death.

Release from the one-hand stranglehold

If you can break free from an aggressor's grip, you have a chance of being able to run to safety or to turn the aggression around in your favour. One of the simplest release techniques to master is breaking free from the one-hand strangle-hold. This is where the aggressor has one hand around your throat to hold you, usually keeping you in position whilst he hits you with his free hand. Using the heel of your hand, the technique is to hit the wrist of the aggressor hard enough to dislodge his hand from your throat, while at the same time lifting your knee sharply to hit him in the groin. By doing this, you will have weakened his throat grip on you and, as he realizes that your knee is aimed at his groin, he will pull back, bending his body away from you to try to avoid a groin injury. At this point he will be off-balance, and you can either run to safety, or head-butt him in the face. If you have managed to connect with your knee, you may have injured him enough to give you the advantage to incapacitate him.

Release from the two-handed stranglehold

With the two-handed stranglehold, the aggressor will be facing you with both hands grabbing you around the throat; his thumbs will be pressed against your windpipe, restricting your breathing. Cross your right hand over the top of his arms and grab his right hand. Push your thumbnail deep into the flesh between his thumb and first finger. At the same time, curl your fingers around his hand and pull the hand away, twisting it as if to sprain the wrist, so that his palm is forced to face upwards. As you are carrying out this manoeuvre, bring your left hand up to his right elbow; your thumb should go under the elbow and the fingers should hold the back of the elbow, forcing it up to lock it. As he releases his grip and is off-balance, keep a firm hold of him with both hands and turn sharply to your right, twisting the whole of his wrist and arm against the joints. Push down with the elbow grip until he bends forward. You are now in a position to deliver him a powerful blow to the back of his elbow with the edge of your hand, or alternatively use all of your weight to collapse the elbow by landing your left knee on it.

Release from a hair-hold from the rear

As soon as you feel your hair being gripped, lift both of your hands over your head and tightly grip the aggressor's wrist. As you do so, drop your body slightly and turn to your right quickly. As the grip breaks, keep your wrist grip and twist the arm, forcing the aggressor to bow down. Take the weight of your body on your left leg and deliver a powerful kick to his face, aiming for the nose.

Strangle-hold

Either approach the aggressor from behind or turn him around so that he is facing away from you. Throw your left arm around his throat so that your inner arm bone is flattening his windpipe. Lift up your right arm and grip your biceps with your left hand. Push your right hand behind the aggressor's head and force it forward, so increasing the windpipe's constriction; the aggressor will soon lapse into unconsciousness. If you can drop to your knees in a quick movement and continue to exert the pressure, you will dislocate the aggressor's neck and kill him outright.

STRANGLE HOLD

STOPPING A KNIFE ATTACKER

Angling the chair so that the legs are presented in a diamond shape ensures that the aggressor is hit with at least two legs, whereas when running at him with the legs squared, the legs may go either side of his body and miss the vital areas.

Knives are often used by aggressors because they are easily obtained and can be carried without detection. If you are faced with a knife attacker, you can be absolutely sure that the aggressor is out to inflict as much damage as he possibly can. Use a chair held close to your chest to defend yourself against the initial attack. When the opportunity arises, straighten your arms and run at the aggressor, aiming the uppermost legs at his face and the lower legs at his upper chest.

The killer blow

In many cases, you may only have one chance to overpower an aggressor. In these cases you need a blow that will do the most damage, even if you are not very strong or are not used to fighting. Using a tightly rolled newspaper or even a matchbox held in a fist so that the item protrudes a little from the thumb side of the fist will deal a devastating blow that will send a shock wave deep into the aggressor's head and smash his facial bones. Deliver it with a wide, strong swing and aim to hit him anywhere between the cheekbone and the lower jaw. If it lands full force on the lower jaw bone, it will break it and put it out of line to such an extent that it can kill the opponent.

The ear-slap

If your hands are free and the aggressor is in striking distance, cup your hands, keeping your fingers tightly closed to make a seal, and deliver a blow as fast and hard as possible to both ears at the same time. The blow will compress air in the inner ears, bursting the eardrums and causing a loss of balance and momentary loss of co-ordination. Even one hand has a devastating effect, and can give you the opportunity to run to safety.

EAR SLAP

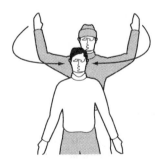

EAR SLAP - Delivering this blow with both hands at the same time will cause severe pain and inner-ear injury. The aggressor will have to let go of you, giving you the opportunity to run away or to deliver another debilitating blow such as finger jabs to the eyes.]

Disarming a short gun

A gun ready to fire and the aggressor's finger already around the trigger may seem to be impossible to live through, but with speed of thought and action you can turn what seems like a helpless situation into a winning one. Firstly, ask yourself why you have not been shot already. This has to be because the aggressor is waiting for some reason, and that is in your favour. Even though you think he is hesitating, do make sure you work on the basis that he will pull that trigger sooner or later. If he has gone to the trouble of pulling a gun on you, he must be desperate. Let him see that you are scared – if he tells you to move, do so; do not aggravate the situation. If he can see that you are scared and carrying out his every instruction without hesitation, he may feel more comfortable in getting close enough to you to allow you to disarm him.

As soon as you have the opportunity, quickly hit and grab his wrist, turning slightly to your side so that if the gun is discharged there is less of a target to hit. In any event, use your free hand to grasp the gun and turn it further away from you, twisting the aggressor's hand and forcing him to release his grip. As you do this, distract him from holding onto the weapon by delivering a knee to his groin and head-butting him as he bends forward to avoid the groin contact. Once you have the gun, do not give him the opportunity to disarm you!

DISARMING A SHORT WEAPON

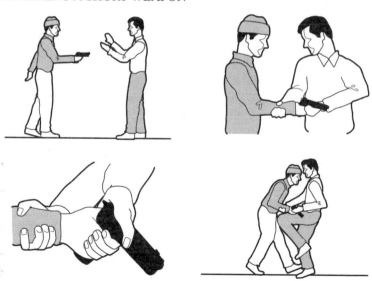

DISARMING A SHORT WEAPON - Short-barrelled guns are designed to be used in confined spaces. Wait until the aggressor is up close to you before you disarm him. Once you have the gun, use it to kill him.

13. Acts of terror

There was a time not too long ago when the likelihood of the average person being involved in any form of terrorist attack was very remote indeed. Nowadays, however, there are very few areas where a terrorist will not strike; there is an increasing chance that you will be subjected to some form of terrorist attack or unwittingly used in some way or other.

The events of 11 September 2001 – terrible though they undoubtedly were – cannot be seen as the end of terrorism: they were, in fact, the next stage. And in terms of terrorism as an act of violence and intimidation to achieve a goal, this was a terrorist plan that accomplished all that it set out to. It woke the world up to terrorism, and terrorists' total disregard for innocent people.

Hijacking
Having started with 11 September, I think it is worth looking at the best way to survive a hijacking, although I should point out that the taking of a vehicle for the sole purpose of using it as a weapon of destruction is not strictly speaking a hijacking. As a terrorist act, a hijacking supposes that the perpetrators have demands, and have selected a passenger vehicle to use its passengers as hostages as a tool of negotiation to realize those demands, or as a way of gaining the public's and media's interest in their cause and to gain a world-wide audience.

In respect of the 11 September attack, you can do no better than the brave passengers of United Airlines Flight 93, and seize the opportunity to fight with all your strength to overpower your attackers (see the section on *Self-Defence*).

For many years now, the governments of the world have made it known that they will not give in to hijackers' demands; consequently, hijackers' demands have not been met, and the desired result has not been fully attained. This tactic has caused the majority of hijacked passengers and crews to undergo long periods of high stress – often resulting in their eventual release, but in some cases their death.

In terms of survival, this is a very difficult area. The natural enemies found in the outdoor survival situation are replaced with the more difficult enemy: the unpredictable human animal. Even so, the basics of survival are the same, and you will benefit from knowledge, confidence, physical and psychological condition, a sense of humour and the will to survive. Throughout the encounter, the usual survival priorities of protection, location, water and food still apply. But your best approach will be to adopt as low a profile as possible.

It is vital that right at the start you quickly assess the type of hijacking you are involved in, and ascertain the politics and religious beliefs of the hijackers or the actual extremist group they belong to. Generally, you will be told the politics and the aims and objectives of the hijackers at an early stage. It is possible that your politics, beliefs or nationality may not be in conflict with those of the hijackers, in which case your chances of living through the forthcoming ordeal are slightly higher than those of a passenger whose ideals do conflict. If it comes to choosing who should be executed to prove a point, then it is more likely that the chosen one will be someone against whom the hijackers have some personal grudge. If you are unfortunate enough to be in conflict with the hijackers through simply being from the wrong place or time, then the preferred method of surviving is to adopt a low profile in the hope that someone else less astute will inadvertently draw attention to themselves and away from you.

Terrorists do not choose their victims on a first-come, first-served basis; it is more likely that those chosen will be the ones who make themselves known. Therefore your course of action is to avoid being singled out at all costs. Obviously it is difficult not to react when you are being treated in a violent or uncomfortable manner. At the very least, you can expect to be kept for some time with your hands on your head. This may seem quite a civilized way of keeping order, but sitting in this position for long periods causes severe pain in the shoulders, neck, upper arms and chest. Complaining or moving position should be avoided, as these actions will only serve to single you out. The best course is to suffer in silence and allow other, less-knowledgeable detainees to take up the issues if they choose to. Their attention to the problem will either bring the situation to a sympathetic ear or will serve to begin the selection process of the first victim – either way, the problem will not be yours.

Bindings are unpleasant and cause severe pain and discomfort. Your only respite will be by flexing your muscles or expanding your limbs when you get the chance (see *Kidnapping*).

Unfortunately, the situation may develop to the point where the terrorists are becoming increasingly violent towards you. At this stage, there is very little you can do, and you will have to take it as best you can. If you are absolutely sure that you are in a position to overpower the terrorists, or you are in no doubt that they are about to take your life, then fight! (see section on *Self-Defence*). If not, resistance may well make the situation worse. The best method of dealing with it is to show pain when it hurts: to show pain too early can cause the aggressor to become impatient; to show arrogance by trying to display how 'hard' you are will almost certainly end in your being beaten to death.

Playing games with your captors by displaying your arrogance and thereby gaining their respect only happens in movies. If you decide to play games, try to build a relationship with the terrorists – if you can get a good rapport, it is much better and often leads to survival (see *The Psychology of Self-Defence*).

Your overall bearing will have an effect on the way you are ultimately treated. Some people have what can only be described as a 'military style' about them; they walk upright, with an air of authority. You should avoid this approach at all costs as the terrorists, who will be used to the police and military, may well take you for a soldier or undercover operator. On the other hand, if you sit slouching and displaying a seemingly unconcerned attitude, you may be seen as arrogant and be singled out as a possible troublemaker. Being aware of your body language and adjusting it accordingly is a very important skill (see the section on *Effective Communication*).

Communication, or the lack of it, is a difficult area and can only be decided at the time. In essence, your non-verbal communication will begin the process. The way you stand, the way you use your eyes and facial expression can show dislike, mistrust, hate and many other emotions, which can give the terrorist an impression that is either threatening to him or not. It is difficult to get the balance right – to show hate for your captors is as provocative as showing compassion in some situations. Inevitably, any communication will begin to single you out and thereby defeat the object of your keeping a low profile. The ideal way of dealing with this aspect of survival is to avoid deep eye-to-eye contact – which does not mean to say that you should avoid eye contact altogether, as this will be seen as antagonistic. If you have to look at your aggressor, then do so; to cast your gaze elsewhere will be seen as an act of defiance.

The chances are that you will be unaware of your ultimate destination and of the demands set by the terrorists to secure your release. What will be apparent to you is the amount of time you have spent on the ground. If the hijackers are experienced, they will insist that the aircraft undertakes a number of journeys from airport to airport on their way to the ultimate destination; these short halts reduce the risk of an armed assault by the authorities. As you can appreciate, before an armed rescue can be launched, the appropriate authorities have to consider all the options, try to bring the hijack to a non-violent conclusion by negotiation, and fully explore the legal and political implications of an armed assault; this all takes time. The decision-making process may involve people from different countries and with opposite views, and the chances of them being immediately available and in a position to make informed decisions is very slim – it may take two or three days before they can get together.

Even after the political decisions have been made, the ultimate decision to use force to bring the hijacking to an end would only be given after all other efforts have failed and the lives of the hostages are seriously at risk. Another consideration is that the country in which the hijackers have finally made their demands may not have a properly trained anti-terrorist force or any trained personnel to deal effectively with the situation. Specialists may have to be brought in to oversee the whole of the rescue operation, and they may eventually be called upon to effect an armed response. If the hijacking has been going on for some time and the aircraft has made a number of flights, then it will have been followed and monitored. The information gathered needs to be correlated and assessed, and again this all takes time.

Even an experienced team has its limitations. For example, the aircraft may have been flown through restricted airspace, and the observers' aircraft may not have been allowed to follow. If the plane is constantly flying from place to place, then the team will monitor its fuel consumption and plan an assault on the basis of the plane having to refuel at the next stop. With this information, they can identify possible refuelling facilities and plan an assault at several likely locations. These locations may be narrowed down by possible destination airports signalling ground problems that effectively stop any aircraft from landing because of safety fears; alternatively, airport authorities may not grant landing rights, or may cause obstructions on the runways. The result is that the plane will have to land at a facility that has already been selected by the assault team as the best option for a rescue; in these situations, the actual assault can be launched relatively quickly.

As a gesture of goodwill, some hostages are generally released early in a hijack. If you are fortunate enough to be in this group, the authorities will want to interview you about your ordeal as soon as possible so that they can gain a better idea of the threat. During your time as a hostage, make a mental note of the events and a description of the terrorists, their ages, the weapons they have, where they usually stand and any specific idiosyncrasies. This information will be of great importance to the negotiators and other officials.

If you have not been fortunate enough to be released early, then the chances of being involved in some form of armed conflict will have increased. You may be lucky and be released without harm, but throughout the hijacking you must be alert to the possibility of conflict and prepare yourself to react in a positive way the moment the assault starts. Most units trained in anti-terrorist work will begin an attack using stun grenades; when these explode, they cause a shock wave that affects your hearing, balance and co-ordination for a short period. The worst thing you can do is to try to run: in the first place, the effect of the stun grenade will keep you off-balance, making running difficult and, secondly, you are likely to run straight into a hail of bullets. The best plan is to get down onto the floor, thereby allowing the *mêlée* to go on above you. If possible, remain in this position until you are ordered to move – hopefully by a friendly force. In the event of your having to move because of a hazard such as a fire, then stay low and if possible evacuate the aircraft. Once outside stay down and, if you can, get clear of the aircraft. If you are not sure which way to go, lie down with your hands outstretched so that the authorities can see that you are not armed; stay in this position until you are told to move.

There is a chance that your survival has been due to your maintaining a low profile and, in doing so, you may have stood by while others have been executed. Afterwards, you may feel a sense of guilt as you reflect on your ordeal and try to come to terms with your lack of action to assist the victims. What you must realize is that you cannot hold yourself responsible for the actions of others.

Much of the advice contained in the above section on *Hijacking* can be used in all aspects of face-to-face terrorist acts where your freedom and rights are taken from you.

Kidnapping

Kidnapping hostages is a terrorist act that has been used the world over. Much of the advice given in the text on surviving a hijacking can be used in a hostage situation, although obviously it is completely impossible to keep a low profile when you are the only one involved.

The fact that you have not been killed in the first place suggests that the kidnappers have some reason to keep you alive – for the time being, anyway. This fact is the key to your early survival: because they have a reason to keep you alive, they will hesitate before taking your life. From the moment you are aware of your kidnap, you should be looking for a way to escape – the longer you are held captive, the more difficult it is to escape. In the first moments of capture, you will probably be in an area where there is an element of normality, so if you can effect your escape at this early stage, the chances are that you can find salvation and help locally. However, once you have been taken away from the area, you will probably not know where you are or who you can trust if you do escape.

Once the kidnappers have detained you, they are likely to restrain you by tying you up and gagging you. Even when this has been done, there is a chance of a quick escape. The way you do this is to present parts of your body to be bound in such a way that the binding can be loosened afterwards. Present your hands in front of your body by keeping the heels of your hands together and slightly cupping them. At the same time, keep your hands close to your body with your elbows pushed out, which causes your wrists to part. Binding you in this position allows you to straighten your arms later, which will push your wrists together, thus loosening the bindings. Flattening your hands palm to palm will further loosen them until you can wriggle free. If a mouth gag is being used, push your chin on your chest and puff your cheeks out; if at all possible, also keep your teeth tightly closed. These positions will again allow you to loosen your bindings when you draw your chin, open your teeth and stretch your neck to its full extent. If your hands are being tied behind your back, present them thumb to thumb with your palms facing outwards and your arms slightly bent. Once again, try to ensure that there is a good gap between your wrists. Turning your hands palm to palm and drawing them up your back will loosen the binding and allow you to slip out. Then you may be in a position to surprise your captors by escaping from them at a time when they are complacent, believing that you could not escape. Running out of a building into a street full of local people will bring immediate attention to your problem – it is unlikely that your kidnappers would dare to retake you in full view of the general public.

If you have not had a chance to escape in the very early stages of your captivity, the chances are that you will be moved from the initial kidnap site in the back of a vehicle – quite often a car. If you have a mouth gag, you will probably be made to lie in the well between the front and rear seats and covered over so that you cannot be seen. If you are not gagged, you may be sat in the rear of the vehicle with a guard. In both cases, think about escaping by loosening your bindings and quickly opening the door and jumping out as the vehicle starts moving (clearly, you would be foolish to attempt this if the vehicle is travelling at speed). But in the middle of a city or town, the chances are that the vehicle will often have to slow down for other road users. An ideal time to jump is when the vehicle is pulling away from a set of traffic lights: force the door open and throw yourself out of the near-side, making sure you don't throw yourself under a passing vehicle. You will certainly suffer cuts and bruises, but they are far less than the problems you will encounter from becoming a hostage. Once the vehicle has left built-up areas. it will probably be travelling at great speed and passing through areas where there are few people. Then the chances are that you will have to wait a very long time before you can spot another window of opportunity.

Surviving until the window of opportunity presents itself, or until you are released, will be your priority. In the early stages, hostages are often very confused and have trouble coming to terms with their predicament. They obviously mistrust their captors, and in group hostage situations there are periods when there is a mistrust of one's self and of colleagues. Keeping the mind positively active is a very important part of hostage survival: to allow the mind to dwell on negative thoughts will inevitably sap the will to survive. Never let the mind relax. This is best accomplished by having a personal project, such as building an imaginary lavish garden, a luxury home, a rocket – in fact, anything that is productive. In a hostage situation, the one thing that the captors cannot take away from you is your thoughts – the inner you. You must keep this part of you totally in your control at all times.

In isolation, with minimum human contact, there is a feeling of hopelessness that you have to overcome. The only emotional support for you is you! Living without affection of any kind can eat away at you, and it is this that you must always guard against. Political hostages are often forced to make public statements, admitting to a crime against the state or its people, or denouncing a country, its people and/or its politics. Not agreeing with the views of your captors and not wanting to make any statements is in some ways accepted, and so the isolation, tiredness and uncertainty are used to wear you down to a stage where you will say and do almost anything. The captors will try everything to domineer, but to completely domineer they have to break you. A way of accomplishing this is to threaten to take your life. Having the courage to accept that they may well kill you and being able to live with that thought without fear takes away the most powerful lever the captors have to force you to conform, to do as they say. Quite often when hostages get to this stage and have come to terms with the possibility of their death, they have turned the tables on their captors. It can become a battle of wills: the captor determined to break the hostage, to rule not just the body but the mind as well; the hostage, accepting that there is little he can do to stop the punishments on his body, but resisting every attempt to capture his mind. In these situations, the captor loses if he takes the hostage's life. The result is that the captor will continue to try to break the hostage, making sure he does not die for fear of failure.

The chances are that you will be held in a building, probably not far from a busy street or near to someone who can help you. You must constantly review the best action to take to survive your ordeal; you have to be sure that to escape is in your best interests. It may be the case that you are being held in quite decent surroundings and being treated properly – perhaps because negotiations are going on to secure your release. There certainly will be some action being taken to help you from outside agencies, but only you can decide whether or not your life is at risk and whether escape is a realistic possibility.

Having decided that your survival will depend on escaping, you should prepare and plan your escape if at all possible. If not, you will have to play a waiting game until the opportunity arises. Your route out of the building may well include having to drop from a window, low roof or wall, and being able to drop and land properly will lessen the risk of recapture due to injury. When faced with a high drop, look for the softest place to land – if you can, try to cushion your fall with clothing, bedding or other soft material. Where you can, ease yourself over the edge of the drop, making sure you are facing the building, keeping one hand holding on until your arm is fully stretched; look down and pick a safe spot to land. While still holding on, place your free hand on the wall and push yourself away from the wall as you let go. The push should be enough to keep you clear of the building during your descent (it should also spin you a little so that you face away from the building). Keep looking at the spot on which you intend to land. Keep your ankles and knees pressed together and your legs slightly bent at the knees. Push your chin onto your chest and keep your teeth together. Pull both of your hands up to the side of your head, and position yourself to land with the balls of the feet landing first: do not land heels first. As soon as your feet hit the ground, force your knees to the side. This move, combined with the forward force of your body, will turn you in such a way that you will roll onto the floor, thereby spreading the impact. By doing this, your body will gradually take the force of the landing and greatly reduce the chance of injury. Once you are safely on the ground, make good your escape.

ESCAPING FROM BUILDINGS

Having decided that your survival depends on escaping, the last thing you want is to sustain an injury on your way out. Being able to drop from a height in a controlled way will lessen the risks.

Tips to avoid being kidnapped

- Be aware that you could be a target, and avoid drawing undue attention to yourself
- If you are in a foreign country, dress down and avoid any conflict or debate, especially on the subjects of politics, religion and race
- Do not drive around alone, especially in a local hire car or a car showing foreign licence plates
- Only use approved taxicabs
- When you are on foot, face oncoming traffic; this will lessen the risk of kidnappers coming up from behind you in a car without you knowing
- Change your daily routines regularly to make it difficult for anyone to plan your kidnapping.

Terrorist bombings

One of the terrorist's main weapons is the bomb – usually home-made with very sophisticated timing and detonation devices. I say 'usually' because there are so many different terrorist groups, many of whom get their weapon systems from sympathetic governments, and as such may also use military mines and other devices. Nevertheless the end result is the same: they kill and maim people!

The way in which terrorists choose to deliver their bombs differs from organization to organization. In some cases, suicide bombers will deliver and detonate their bomb while they are wearing it. Others will use a vehicle, driving it into position and either detonating it there and then or leaving it to be detonated at a later time by a timer, command wire or radio signal. In many cases, terrorists will issue a warning prior to detonation, and in these situations your survival will depend on how quickly you move away from the target area. As soon as you suspect, or are told, that there is a bomb in the area, move away without hesitation. If you are not sure where the bomb is, take precautions. The best way to do this is to leave any building you are in and lie face-down outside. If you can quickly get a good distance away from buildings and into a large open space, then do so. If not, lie against one of the building's outside walls and tuck yourself well into it. Cover your ears, and keep your face on the floor and turned slightly towards the building. Make sure that there are no loose or easily moved pieces of equipment that can be blown at you when the bomb detonates – such as rubbish bins, post boxes, motorcycles and so on. If any of these objects is nearby, move to another location. If you are close by when the bomb is detonated, you will feel the heat of it and also the oxygen being pulled out of your lungs. The shock-waves will spread quickly, destroying most things in their immediate path and lessening in power as they radiate away. Close to the ground, the waves should be relatively less violent – the building will absorb some of the shock and bounce other waves away from you. Having survived the initial blast, stay where you are until you are absolutely sure that there is no chance of a second explosion. If the buildings are so badly damaged that they are unstable and falling down, stay where you are. Generally, the tops of buildings fall away from the foundations, leaving a relatively safe zone of a metre (3 yards) or so between building and debris. Following the bombing and subsequent collapse of the building, rescue teams will soon search through the wreckage. If you have taken notice of the advice given in this book, you can signal effectively by blowing your whistle (see section on *Attracting Attention*).

BOMB BLAST FALLING BUILDING

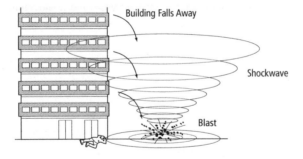

Having survived the initial blast, the main priority will be to keep yourself alive until help arrives.

Letter and parcel bombs

These types of terrorist packages, along with the threat of chemical and biological agents being sent to targets through the postal system, are designed to kill or incapacitate when they are opened. If for any reason you are suspicious, treat your suspicion with respect and carry out immediate action to safeguard yourself and those around you. Survival is about acting appropriately and responding positively. If your instinct is wrong, there is nothing to fear and everyone involved will understand that your actions could well have been justified and have saved lives.

Being able to spot the signs of a potential threat is the first part of your survival. Suspect packages and letters may be delivered by hand, and either posted through the letterbox or left nearby. If this is not something that regularly happens, then it should heighten your suspicion. Suspect package and letters delivered through the post are often posted in another country. Taking note of the stamps and postmarks of unsolicited mail can give you a good indication of potential trouble. Quite often, for example, there will be a disparity in the cost of postage – such as more stamps being used than are necessary. The delivery name and address may also be slightly incorrect or hand-written with letters and numerals that are obviously foreign; mis-spellings and poor writing technique are also common indicators. Packages may be heavily wrapped with a large amount of tape, while packages and envelopes can be grease-stained and/or smell of something resembling marzipan or almonds. Packages are also often much heavier than you would expect for their size, while letters and packages may be uneven in their weight and distribution.

Once you have decided that you are dealing with a suspect device, leave the area immediately, making sure that any other innocent people are not left behind. If you are indoors, open all the windows and doors. At this point, do not switch any electrical equipment or lights on or off, or activate any fire alarms. Under no circumstances should you examine any suspect devices: this is a job for experts only.

NBC

NBC is the term used to indicate weapons or defences that fall into one of three categories: nuclear, biological or chemical. Although they are regularly talked about as if they are one and the same, in fact they are as separate as any other different type of weapon system such as firearms and knives. Both have the potential to inflict injury and death, but both need to be considered in totally separate ways.

There are those who believe that NBC weapons will never be exploited by terrorists. However, as I stated at the beginning of this section, no one can predict what terrorists will do next. Up until the 11 September attacks and their aftermath, the majority of experts believed that terrorist organizations did not have the technical knowledge to use anthrax as a terrorist weapon, but now they have shown that they do! There was a time when the world powers believed that terrorists would not be in a position to deliver a realistic chemical attack, but the release of a nerve agent in Tokyo's underground railway system proved them wrong. The world now expects further attacks of biological and chemical agents. Many thousands of people involved in anti-terrorist work throughout the world also expect terrorists to exploit the nuclear threat – it really is only a matter of time.

As a result of recent events, it would be impossible to write a modern book on survival techniques without including some reference to NBC.

NBC protection

Throughout the world, countries have developed NBC products as weapons of war. Because of this, defence against these weapons has been largely designed to equip fighting troops to continue in war when NBC attacks have already been carried out. This has meant that the majority of the world's civilian population have no equipment issued to them in the event of a sudden attack, and very few designs are civilian user-friendly. Many people have purchased their own NBC protection from retail outlets that specialize in ex-military stock. Obviously, there is a wide range of NBC protection clothing and equipment available, as each country that has developed this equipment has chosen its own particular design. Nevertheless, in essence all protection includes a respirator, suit, gloves and footwear. The majority will give some protection from biological and chemical agents, as well as protecting the wearer from the effects of beta and alpha rays following a nuclear explosion.

Respirators

There are many designs, but all work on the principle of using a filter to clean the polluted air. When properly fitted, the respirator is sealed against the wearer's skin and gives complete protection to the face and respiratory organs, although the filter system has to be changed periodically (this can usually be done without having to remove the respirator). The life of filters differs widely, and the supply of replacements should be considered when a respirator is acquired. If you do purchase a respirator, practise changing the filter regularly.

NBC clothing

The material used in the manufacture of protective clothing is usually lightweight, flame-retardant and impregnated with a layer of chemicals that resists penetration; the suit material is also usually non-woven. This design allows liquids on the outer skin to spread and thereby speeds up the natural evaporation process. Often there is also a thin layer of charcoal, which is steam activated and counteracts any hazard posed by agents being delivered in vapour form.

NBC gloves

Some suits have gloves designed as an integral part of the suit. Others – such as the UK's preferred design – have a neoprene outer glove as an impenetrable layer, with a soft cotton inner glove for comfort.

NBC footwear

Normal footwear – no matter how robust – will not provide protection against the penetrative power of NBC agents and rays. You will need purpose-built footwear. Quite often, NBC footwear will be of an overboot design moulded from tough butyl rubber. As with all the protective kits, these have a relatively short life, and have to be changed regularly.

Personal decontamination and detector kits

There are personal decontamination and detector kits on the market, which usually contain either a puffer and container or a sachet of powder known as Fuller's Earth. If a person becomes contaminated, the Fuller's Earth is sprinkled onto the liquid, which it mops up from the skin and holds in the powder in a harmless state.

Detector kits determine whether or not agents have been released. There are two main types of detector papers: the single colour, which is grey and turns dark blue or black when exposed to liquid agents; and the more sophisticated three-colour paper, which is off-white and changes to red when in contact with a blister agent, yellow with non-persistent nerve agents, and green with persistent nerve agents. Agents that are released into the atmosphere in vapour form are detected with the use of a detector that sniffs the air, known as an RSD (residual vapour detector).

Chemical agents

Agents in this category will kill, seriously injure or incapacitate by physiological effects.

The delivery of this type of agent is as wide-ranging as a terrorist's imagination. The dissemination of the chemicals can take one or more of the following forms: it can be dispersed as a liquid, in splashes or in droplets; in gaseous form as a result of the liquid's rapid evaporation, (often used to deliver mustard gas); as a fine liquid spray; or as minute solid particles which cause a haze, fog or smoke effect (an aerosol).

There is evidence to show that terrorists have considered using crop-spraying aircraft as a way of delivering large quantities of this type of agent onto a selected target.

Once released over the target, the duration of effectiveness is difficult to determine. Weather conditions and climatic variations will affect dispersal to varying degrees, depending on the temperature and the strength and direction of the wind. The likely effectiveness can be determined by categorizing the agents as persistent or non-persistent.

Non-persistent
These agents can be delivered as liquids, vapours or aerosols, and evaporate very quickly. The ensuing cloud of vapour is carried on the wind and is dispersed by diffusion. This type of agent delivery is very effective in relatively confined spaces where there is a flow of air, such as an underground railway system.

Persistent
These agents are usually in solid form, but also can be delivered as a liquid. Once they have been released, they will remain in the target area. As well as the initial problem of contamination, there are the long-lasting effects as the chemicals slowly evaporate.

Agents and their effects
To be effective, a chemical agent has to enter the body, which can happen in one of three ways: by breathing in the agent; by absorption through the pores of the skin or through the eyes; or by ingestion, swallowed with food or water.

For many years, intelligence sources have seen the infiltration of fresh-water supplies by terrorists as a way of potentially delivering a large dose of killer agents and life-threatening micro bacteria.

Nerve agents
In the absence of adequate protection, these agents can enter the body by

any of the above routes. Their purpose is to disrupt the body's natural functions, causing the loss of muscle control. As the function of inhalation is largely muscle-assisted, the ability to breathe is greatly impaired. The nerve agents cannot be detected by human senses, and the first indication of contamination will be the development of symptoms. In the early stages, there will be an increase in saliva production, a running nose, tightness of the chest and blurred vision. The problems develop into severe headaches, dizziness and an increase in perspiration, while the most dangerous stage is that of vomiting and nausea.

Nerve agent has already been used by terrorists, when it was released into the Tokyo underground railway system. In this attack the nerve agent sarin, which is both colourless and virtually odourless, was released by a terrorist cult known as Aum Shinrikyo on three underground trains during the rush-hour in Tokyo, Japan. The nerve agent was concealed in lunch-boxes and soft-drinks containers, which were placed on the trains' floors and released by the terrorists as they left the train by puncturing the containers with umbrellas. As a result of this simple attack, 5500 people were infected and 11 lost their lives.

A pre-treatment known as NAPS (Nerve Agent Pre-treatment Set) is available. This is a 14-day treatment consisting of two seven-day packs of 30mg pyridostigmine tablets, which should be taken every eight hours prior to an expected attack.

Blood agents (hydrogen, cyanide)

These agents have the effect of reducing the body tissue's ability to absorb oxygen supplied in the blood. In very high concentrations, the effect can be rapid respiratory failure.

The routes of entry into the body are either by inhalation – the most effective – or by absorption. However, the wearing of an NBC suit and respirator gives complete protection.

The effects resulting from contamination can appear within a very short period. The amount of agent inhaled will determine the severity of the symptoms, which are dizziness, nausea, severe headache and difficulty in breathing. This breathing impairment may cause the contaminated person to remove the respirator in an effort to improve his breathing, but doing this will certainly result in death. If you keep the respirator properly fitted, the symptoms will wear off.

Choking agents (chlorine, phosgene)

These agents are only effective if they are inhaled. The effect of inhalation is to cause large amounts of fluid to be produced in the lungs, inducing a drowning effect. Some of the agents work very quickly, and it is essential to put on the respirator as soon as possible to avoid contamination. If there has been any agent inhalation, the casualty will experience a shortage of breath and bouts of coughing. In severe cases, the lack of oxygen will cause a rapid state of unconsciousness followed by death. Initial choking is not an indication of the severity of contamination. In some cases, there can initially be a quick recovery followed by a relapse within 48 hours.

Blister agents (sulphur, mustard, lewisite, phosgene, oxime)

These agents are extremely persistent; they evaporate, giving off invisible vapours, which are then carried considerable distances by the wind and air currents. They penetrate normal clothing and skin, with the eyes being particularly susceptible – even a small amount will irritate them, to the point where they water profusely and eventually close (with larger doses, there is a risk of permanent blindness). If inhaled, the agent causes a dry burning throat accompanied by coughing, and a fever develops. The first external sign is a reddening of the skin accompanied by a burning sensation, and blisters will appear under the armpits and around the groin.

Realistically the only effective protection is a purpose-made NBC suit.

Incapacitating agents

These agents are designed to affect the mind. Mood changes, and difficulty in concentrating and decision-making, are the first signs of contamination. Motor-neurone skills are also affected, so the contaminated person experiences difficulty in standing and walking – these effects are evident even with small doses of the agent. However, the time taken for the effects to become apparent is unpredictable, and can range from one hour to several days.

Biological agents

There are numerous biological agents that could be used as weapons to kill, incapacitate or terrorize large numbers of people. However, it is widely believed that the agents described in this section are more likely to be used in terrorist attacks. To date, little is known about the effects of widespread contamination from biological agents if they were delivered in an aerosol form. Aerosol is the most effective way to cause widespread contamination, but the difficulties in perfecting this technique mean that terrorist groups will probably use easier methods such as polluting water supplies, attacks through the post and limited release in confined areas.

Many of the early symptoms of infection by biological agents resemble other symptoms of everyday diseases such as the common cold and influenza. Whether or not one should seek immediate medical assistance if symptoms do occur should be dictated by the balance of the probability of having been exposed to biological agents.

Anthrax

Of all the possible diseases that can be used as a weapon, anthrax is probably the most serious. It has already been used with limited effect by terrorists in the aftermath of 11 September when it was posted in powder form to prominent politicians and killed a few people who inadvertently handled it. Aum Shinrikyo, the terrorist group responsible for the release of sarin in Tokyo (see *Nerve Agents*), has also attempted to deliver anthrax by aerosol. Although this attempt was not successful, it has been seen as a trial, and consequently there is concern that this terrorist group will be able to develop a far more effective system of delivery in the future.

In its natural form, anthrax is usually contracted through contact with affected animals that have ingested the spores from infected ground. There are three methods by which the spores can enter the human body: breathing them in (inhalation); through the skin (cutaneous); and digestion (gastrointestinal).

Symptoms of inhalation resemble those associated with fever – coughing, headache, vomiting, abdominal pains and general weakness. They can last a few hours or days and are followed by a second, more severe fever, difficulty in breathing, profuse sweating and shock. Death can occur within hours.

In the cutaneous method, the agent settles on exposed skin and enters the body through cuts and grazes. The symptoms begin with an initial bump that soon develops into a blister, and later ulcerates and leaks fluid. A black scab forms, falls off and fluid oozes from the skin. Without medical attention, death can occur.

The first symptoms of gastrointestinal entry may be an oral ulcer, or an ulcer forming in the throat. Once it gets into the intestine, the agent causes a general feeling of nausea and severe abdominal pain; blood is present in both vomit and diarrhoea.

Anthrax is odourless and colourless, and is not transmitted from person to person. If you consider that you have been subjected to a terrorist attack, close your mouth, place a handkerchief or other close-woven material over your nose to act as a filter, and move away from the source. If you have been subjected to a powdered form by opening an envelope, for example, then place the package down out of any draughts. If possible, use a fine water spray to dampen the powder, thereby reducing the risk of it blowing around and contaminating other areas, then secure the area. Once you have left the contaminated area, step into a shower or bath fully clothed. Remove your clothing, leaving it in the water, and thoroughly wash your hair and body. If you have open wounds or grazes, use a nailbrush to scrub the wounds clean.

Once you have completed your de-contamination washing, alert the authorities and seek immediate medical help. Anthrax responds well to antibiotics, and there is a very good chance of survival with no ill effects.

Botulism

Botulism is a paralytic illness caused by a toxin. It can be contracted by eating food that is infected by the botulism toxin, by infiltration through a wound infected with botulism, or in the case of infant botulism by consuming the spores of the *botulinum* bacteria. All forms are potentially fatal.

In the early stages, nausea, vomiting and stomach pain are the symptoms. The throat becomes dry, vision is blurred, and swallowing and speech may be affected.

Once the infection takes hold, there is a rapid onset of muscle weakness or paralysis. These symptoms begin in the upper body and head, and move down the arms, trunk and legs. As the toxin takes hold, breathing becomes increasingly difficult. Severe cases can result in respiratory failure. Treatment is by way of antitoxins. If the sufferer can get medical help, they can be placed on a ventilator and with proper nursing care they will slowly recover.

In the survival situation, if you seriously suspect that you have been subjected to botulism poisoning and cannot get medical assistance, you can induce vomiting to clear the infected food, and use an enema to clear the gut (great care should be taken when using improvised enemas).

Pneumonic plague

Plague has been around for more than 2000 years. A disease associated with rats, it has killed millions of people over the ages – between 1898 and 1901, an outbreak in India killed approximately ten million people. Although there is little evidence to suggest that terrorist groups are currently actively pursuing the use of the plague as a weapon, the risk is there.

If this method of attack were to be used, pneumonic plague would be suitable for dispersion in aerosol form. Exposure will cause symptoms of fever, overall fatigue, spitting blood, severe chest pain and coughing. Two to six days after the initial exposure the symptoms increase, and could lead to septic shock and death.

The most successful treatment is well known to medical practitioners, and involves courses of prophylactics.

Smallpox

As well as anthrax, it is universally agreed that bioterrorists are very likely to use smallpox in an attack. Smallpox is feared as a terrorist weapon because of its highly contagious nature. Delivered in aerosol form, the virus sustains itself by spreading from person to person by inhalation. Because of the difficulties in obtaining the smallpox virus, a terrorist would have to obtain a stock from one of the world's rogue states.

Once a person is contaminated, fever develops accompanied by severe headache and back pain. Small red spots develop on the tongue and face, but it can be up to 14 days before these symptoms appear. Two or three days afterwards a rash develops over the face and spreads down the arms and legs, eventually covering the whole body. These small spots develop into blisters, fill with puss and crust over, and there is a great amount of pain as the rash grows and develops. The crusts break in the later stages, and death usually occurs two weeks after the first signs.

Nuclear weapons

It is difficult to imagine that terrorists will ever have the capacity to explode a nuclear bomb, but the fact is that we must assume that they will be in a position to do so one day.

Even a small nuclear explosion will cause mass destruction. Whether people will survive it will be determined by the explosion's size, where it is exploded, the distance you are away from it and your protection. Obviously, surviving the initial detonation is the first problem; thereafter a great deal depends on the effects the explosion has had on you, and on your chances of long-term survival in a post-nuclear environment.

The immediate effects of a nuclear explosion are a blinding flash of light, a wave of heat caused by the explosion's fireball as it burns the gases resulting from the explosion, and a blast of wind travelling at more than 250mph (400kph), along with severe shock waves travelling through the ground.

Looking at the intense light at the time of the initial explosion can cause blindness. It can be temporary, but some people will be permanently blinded. The wave of heat will incinerate anyone in close proximity to the actual blast, and the severity of burning thereafter will be determined by your distance from the explosion. The wind and shock waves will cause debris to be thrown around and buildings to collapse. Injuries will obviously be sustained by anyone caught in the open or within or near damaged and falling buildings. The alpha, beta and gamma rays will cause radiation burning of the skin and internal tissue damage.

When you realize that a nuclear bomb has been detonated, close your eyes and drop to the floor face-down with your hands under your body. You must stay in this position until the explosion has ended and all of the debris has stopped falling. This action will give you some protection against all of the immediate effects. Where possible, stay under cover in underground shelters such as subways or cellars, and keep as much of your skin covered as you possibly can. A full NBC suit gives some protection from the effects of burning.

If you have managed to survive the initial stages, you should evacuate the area as soon as possible.

PART 3
Location

14. Map and Compass

There are two types of map in everyday use: the topographical, and the plan. Both can be used to begin planning and assist in a survival situation.

The topographical map shows both physical and man-made features. Topographical map scale (which I shall explain in detail later) varies from 1:10,000 to 1:25,000. For the purposes of planning the survival or self-rescue operation, the 1:50,000 scale can be used to look at a wide area for location and surveillance, while the 1:25,000 scale gives a good indication of more local features and the shape of the land around the survival area. Both can be used to give map references to indicate a precise location.

The plan map depicts built-up areas in such detail that it even gives street names and other man-made features. Unlike the topographical map, the plan does not show physical details such as the rise and fall of the land. It is a useful aid to planning, and can indicate parks or an open area of land that may be used as cover in an escape-and-evasion situation, and indicates built-up areas where help may be found. Most plan maps also show prominent buildings such as police stations, schools and hospitals.

On the maps, symbols and colours are used to show features in detail. To understand this, it is best if you think of the cartographer's task. In simple terms, the cartographer starts with a plain sheet of paper. The job then is to portray the 'bird's eye view' of the land in a way in which we can all understand. To do this, the cartographer first shows the relief of the terrain – its shape, rise and fall. This is done with the use of contours – imaginary lines on the ground indicating land at the same height above sea level. These lines are placed on the map and show the shape of the land, giving height values in metres.

MAP RELIEF

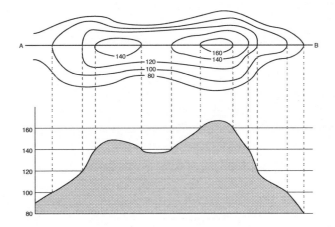

Without knowing how the land lies, you cannot plan a route to safety.

Contours start at sea level. However, on occasions it is necessary to show inland features that are below sea level, such as the bottom of quarries. To express depths below sea level, a system called *bathymetric relief* is used. This employs a contour system similar to that above sea level, except the contours are usually coloured blue. On modern maps the measurements are in metres, but on older ones they are given in fathoms, (1 fathom = 6 feet/1.9m). If bathymetric relief is used on your map, then the datum will be given in the map's marginal information.

Knowing how the land lies constitutes a very important part of the information you need when planning to effect a self-rescue. Understanding the relationship between map and ground only comes with constant practice. At first, the difference between your interpretation of the ground taken from the map and the actual ground will dishearten you, but do not despair; as you become more proficient, your interpretation will become more accurate.

To maintain the accuracy of the map, the cartographer uses scale. Scale is defined as the relationship between the horizontal distance within two known points measured on the ground and the same two points measured on the map. Scales are expressed in ratios – for example, 1:50,000, 1:25,000. This means that one unit on the map represents the stated number of units on the ground. As an example, the scale 1:25,000 means that one centimetre on the map is equal to 25,000 centimetres (2.5

87

kilometres) on the ground. In map-reading, it is important to understand that a change in scale will cause features to be reduced or enlarged proportionately. This means that a feature shown at 1:25,000 scale will be a quarter of the size at 1:100,000 scale, and an eighth of the size at 1:200,000 scale.

To measure horizontal distance, maps carry a graphic linear scale. The zero is set forward from the left of the scale by one full division, which is then sub-divided. When measuring distance using this type of scale, you must always remember to start at the zero and end with the tenths.

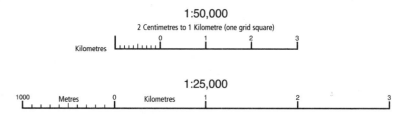

When measuring the route, use a piece of paper to mark the exact route and then measure this against the map linear measure.

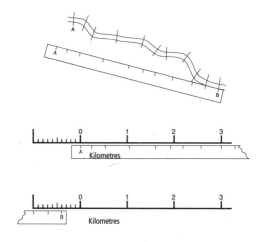

Being able to measure your proposed route will help you to decide how long it will take to complete the journey.

The grid system

Maps are criss-crossed with a series of lines that form squares known as grid squares. A map's grid system provides a method whereby any point can be defined by reference to the lines.

Two main types of grid system are used on maps for land navigation: the Universal Transverse Mercator (UTM), and the British National Grid (BNG). The UTM is the one most often used for military mapping, and covers the whole world except for the polar regions. The BNG covers Great Britain, and is the one used by the Ordnance Survey. Like the UTM, the BNG uses a system based on the Mercator projection, and consists of a series of 100,000-metre squares covering Great Britain; the squares are given identification letters.

Using a map

In a practical situation, the first requirement of a map-reader is to set the map correctly, which can be done in one of two ways: with a compass, or by visual means.

To set a map visually is to turn it until the features depicted on the map correspond with the position of the same features on the ground. Setting the map visually is simple and effective. Using a map of your local area, open it up, keeping the majority of the print the correct way up. In this position the top of the map is northerly. Taking the map outside to practise, choose a position that offers you a good outlook of the area. You need to find a prominent feature on the ground that is easily identifiable on your map, such as a railway bridge, lake, church or other similar feature. Holding the map in front of you, move it around until the map symbols line up with their respective features on the ground.

ORIENTATING THE MAP

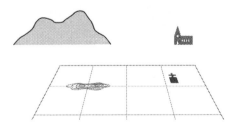

Practice and experience will give you confidence in an emergency.

A common mistake in map-reading is that the user tries to read a map with the print the correct way up – as if you were reading a book or a newspaper - when, in fact, the map can be read from any angle.

Finding direction

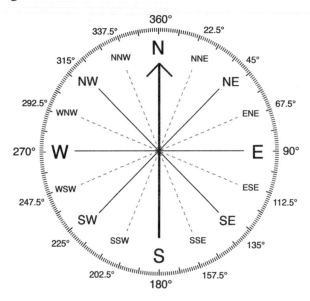

From a chosen location, all features lie on lines of direction from that location; direction is expressed in degrees of a circle, ranging from 0° to 360°. The use of a direction indicator will enhance your overall map skills. Simply place the centre over your position on the map, lining up the north arrow with the north/south lines on your map's grid, and follow the direction lines extending to your feature.

Giving a six-figure map reference

It may well be the case that you will have to give a map reference to your rescuers to indicate your position, or you may have to work to a map reference to locate an area of safety. In both cases your knowledge of map reading will be tested; getting it wrong may well prove costly.

NORTHINGS AND EASTINGS

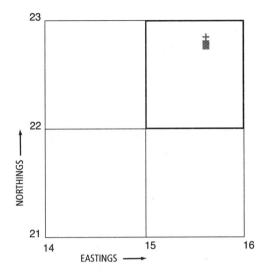

The lines that make up the map's grid are numbered individually by two-figure numbers shown in the map's margin, running from west to east and south to north. To express a particular grid square with reference to its numbers, firstly choose a square and run your finger along an easting (vertical) numbered line from the bottom-left corner of the square, then use the same process along the relevant northing (horizontal) numbered line. In the example above the highlighted square is expressed as 15-22.

PINPOINTING AN EXACT POSITION

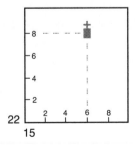

If you wish to find or give a location for a specific feature within the square, such as the church, you will need to break down that square into tenths. The simplest way of doing this is to use a Romer, a scale that sets out the tenths within a grid square. Imagine the grid square divided into tenths horizontally and vertically; now take two imaginary lines both horizontally and vertically to intersect at your feature. This will give you two single numbers which should be included in your four-figure map reference, and are written as 156-228. You now have a six-figure map reference.

Note: the golden rule when giving map references is to give eastings before northings (in other words, the horizontal number first); you can remember this by the fact that E comes before N in the alphabet.

Using grid letters

As previously mentioned, the BNG is divided into lettered squares. Therefore, to make map references absolutely clear, you should have the prefixed map-sheet letters written before the number. You should also record the map serial number so that any follow-up mission can utilize your intelligence correctly.

Using a compass

The basis of a compass is a magnetic needle mounted on a pivot over a compass card which allows it to swing freely until it rests pointing to magnetic north. which is approximately 1,400 miles south of the North Pole, off the Canadian coast. Because of this 'magnetic variation', in map-and-compass work we have to contend with three norths:

- True North – the North Pole
- Grid North – the north shown by the map's grid system
- Magnetic North – the direction in which a magnetized needle points.

A compass enables you to do the following: to find direction and bearings from your position; to follow a direction or bearing accurately; to walk in a straight line; and to return to your starting position.

LIGHTWEIGHT COMPASS

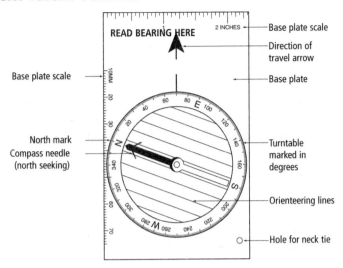

The majority of map-and-compass work today is done using the lightweight Sylva-type compass, so in this book I shall refer to this type only.

Finding direction using bearings

As an exercise, acquire a lightweight compass and go to a suitable location such as your local park or playing fields. Choose a feature some distance away, and hold the compass above the waist in the palm of your hand, ensuring that it is level enough to allow the needle to swing freely. Now point the direction-of-travel arrow at the feature you have chosen. Keeping the compass level and in position, swivel the turntable so that the orienteering arrow falls directly below the north side of the magnetic needle. Read off the bearing given at the base of the direction-of-travel arrow. This is the magnetic bearing to your chosen feature.

Walking a straight line using a compass

Choose a bearing, and adjust your compass so that the chosen bearing is shown in line with the direction-of-travel arrow. Stand directly behind the compass and place yourself so that the north arrow of the magnetic needle is positioned over the orienteering arrow. Place a marker at your feet; now simply follow the direction-of-travel arrow, making sure you keep the magnetic needle in position over the orienteering arrow. Count the paces out, then return to your starting position by simply adding 180° to your original bearing, and follow your 'back bearing' for the same number of paces to your starting position.

Compass errors

Every compass has an individual error and may point a few degrees away from magnetic north; the needle may also not be accurate in relation to the markings on the rose. Every compass should be regularly checked using a known bearing or against another compass of known error. Compass needles are magnetic, and can therefore be attracted by items such as iron, steel, overhead cables, buried pipelines and certain rocks. Even with these errors, a compass is the most useful navigation aid. A common mistake is to discard the compass and rely on your senses (a definite recipe for disaster): always trust your compass.

Using map and compass together

I have already briefly mentioned the different norths. What the navigator needs to understand is the 'Grid Magnetic Variations' – the difference between magnetic north and grid north. Unfortunately, magnetic north moves a little each year. Because of this, maps give the annual change in their marginal information.

Setting a map using a compass

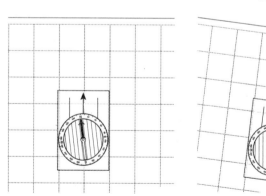
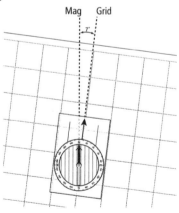

First you need to check the magnetic variation on your map from the marginal information, and adjust your compass. For example, if the magnetic variation is 7° west of grid north, you would have to adjust the compass orienteering arrow by this figure. Then place the compass on the map so that the direction-of-travel arrow lines up with one of the south-north grid lines, with the arrow pointing in the direction of north on the map. Turn the map and compass until the north of the magnetic needle falls over the orienteering arrow.

Finding your exact position

To find your exact position on a map, you need to select two features on the ground that you can identify on your map (such as a hilltop and a church); take a bearing, as explained earlier. This is the magnetic bearing; therefore you need to convert this to a grid bearing before continuing.

To convert a magnetic bearing to a grid bearing, subtract the variation. For example, to convert a magnetic bearing of 340°, we take away the variation – in this case 7° – which means that 333° is the correct bearing. The bearing is now adjusted on the compass to correspond with this value.

Now lay the edge of your compass on the map so that it crosses your chosen feature. Move the compass around until the orienteering lines on the compass are parallel with the south-north grid lines on your map, and pencil in a line: you are now standing somewhere along this line. To determine exactly where, you need to follow the same process using your second feature; the point at which the lines intersect gives you your position.

FINDING YOUR EXACT POSITION

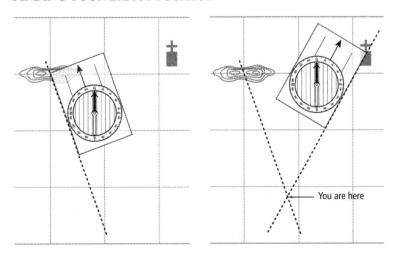

You are here

Remember:
1. Choose two easily identifiable features on your map and the ground
2. Take a magnetic bearing from both
3. Deduct the magnetic variation to give grid bearings
4. Pencil in the lines on your map; the point at which they cross is your actual position.

Using map bearings on the ground

Once you have identified your position you can use your map and compass to move over the ground to a predetermined point (for example, between A and B below). Simply lay the edge of your compass between the two points, and adjust the turntable so that the orienteering lines on the compass lie parallel with the map's grid lines.

Read off the bearing at the base of the direction-of-travel arrow. This is a grid bearing and needs to be converted to a magnetic one before using it to walk by, by adding the magnetic variation: a grid bearing of 310°, becomes a magnetic bearing bearing of 317° in our example. Once you have made this adjustment, hold the compass at waist level, swivel your body until the magnetic needle rests over the arrow, and follow the direction-of-travel arrow to your destination.

TRANSFERRING A MAP BEARING TO A COMPASS BEARING

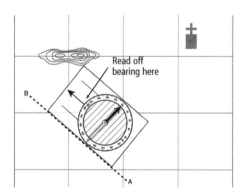

As with all areas of outdoor education, the only way to progress is to spend time outdoors perfecting your skills. Map-and-compass work is the first and most important of these skills, and poor technique accounts for many deaths each year. Never go beyond your capabilities and experience: survival is knowing when to stop, and using common sense.

15. Navigation

In some situations, your chances of survival and rescue may well be enhanced if you move away from your initial location. You may have been shipwrecked and then managed to make a landfall on a remote, tiny island where the food and fresh-water supplies are poor. You may know that another, larger island is to the north, or that there is a better chance of being spotted and eventually rescued if you make your way to busy shipping lanes or areas where commercial shipping and aircraft pass regularly. To be able to make your way to these safer areas, you will need to navigate, or plan a sailing route in a particular direction. Using navigational instruments the task is not too difficult, but in a survival situation (with no instruments) the only way to succeed is to use the navigation aids that nature provides.

The absolute basic navigation rule to remember is that the sun rises from an easterly direction (not due east) and sets in a westerly direction (not due west). If you are in the Northern Hemisphere the sun passes to the south of you, and if you are in the Southern Hemisphere it passes to the north of you.

Direction using the sun
In the greater part of the Northern Hemisphere, the sun is due south at mid-day local time (Greenwich Mean Time in the UK), while in the majority of the Southern Hemisphere the sun is due north at mid-day.

If you have a watch with an analogue dial, you can use it to determine direction. With the watch set at GMT, hold it horizontally and point the hour-hand towards the sun. Now take an imaginary line to bisect the angle between the hour-hand and the 12 o'clock symbol: this line will be pointing true south in the Northern Hemisphere. In the Southern Hemisphere, point the 12 o'clock symbol at the sun. True north then lies midway between the hour-hand and 12 o'clock.

DIRECTION USING THE SUN

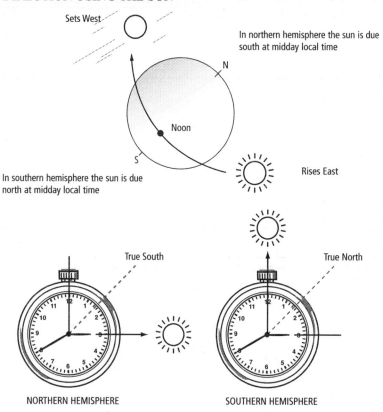

In northern hemisphere the sun is due south at midday local time

In southern hemisphere the sun is due north at midday local time

Rises East

Sets West

Noon

True South

True North

NORTHERN HEMISPHERE

SOUTHERN HEMISPHERE

The watch method is only true at midday local time. For the rest of the time it should only be used as a guide. The watch should be set at GMT not BST. In the northern hemisphere the hour hand is pointed at the sun, then an imaginary line is drawn through the twelve and the mid point between these gives you due south.
In the southern hemisphere, the twelve is pointed at the sun and the mid point between twelve and the hour hand points the direction but this time gives you due north.

If you do not have a watch or you are unsure of the time, you can determine the cardinal compass points and an approximate time by planting a stick around a metre high in level cleared ground. As the sun rises, mark the position of the stick's shadow, which will be cast to the west; you now have the east–west line. During the day, mark the shadow's movement and length; the sun is at its highest at 12 noon, so the shadow will be shortest at mid-day and will be cast pointing true north in the Northern Hemisphere and cast pointing true south in the Southern Hemisphere.

You must consider, however, that from the Equator (0°) to latitude 23.5° north and 23.5° south, the sun's path varies – a variation that is well known and logged, and which is determined by the time of the year. The following table shows you this variation, which must be taken into account when you are plotting any course.

Latitude	Mar 21	May 5	June 22	Aug 9	Sept 23	Nov 7	Dec 22	Feb 5
60°N	89°	55°	37°	55°	89°	122°	140°	122°
30°N	90°	71°	63°	71°	90°	108°	116°	108°
0°Equator	90°	74°	67°	74°	90°	106°	118°	106°
30°S	90°	72°	64°	64°	90°	104°	117°	109°

Being able to determine the sun's exact position will help you to navigate successfully.

NATURES INDICATORS

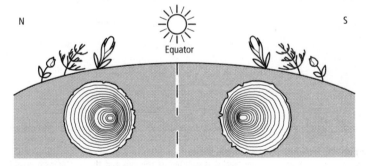

Plants grow towards the sun. When cut, tree rings are closer together on the sunnier side. Bark has more cracks on the sunnier side.

The majority of the earth's plant life is dependent on the sun; as a result, plants have a general tendency to grow better on the sunnier side. The growth rings of trees are closer together on the sunnier side, and the bark has more cracks on the side facing the sun. These are obviously altered by shade and prevailing wind conditions, and cannot be relied on as sole indicators, but in conjunction with other indicators they can give you a general feel for the direction of the Equator.

NORTHEN HEMISPHERE

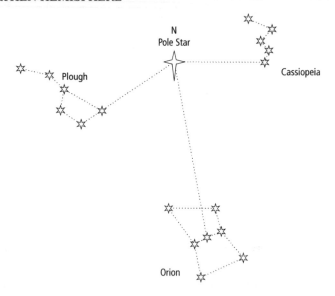

When the sun goes down, the stars take over as the main indicators to navigation. In the Northern Hemisphere, the North or Pole Star indicates true north. You can find this by taking one of the three main star groupings: the Plough (or Great Bear), Orion and Cassiopeia.

In the Southern Hemisphere, you use the Southern Cross as an indicator to determine true south; bring imaginary lines all the way down to the horizon and choose a feature that you can easily identify to navigate towards.

Star gazing is another way of working out direction, although it is less reliable. Select a position looking into space and plant two sticks half a metre (18ins) apart; tie a piece of string between them, or use another thinner stick to span the gap. Choose a star and watch its movements: if it appears to rise, you are facing approximately east; if it falls, it indicates a westerly direction; if it flatly loops to the right, you are facing in a southerly direction; while if it flatly loops to the left it indicates a northerly direction.

SOUTHERN HEMISPHERE

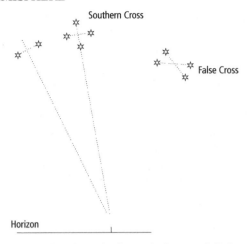

The ancient mariners of the world used stars for thousands of years to help them navigate.

In many areas of the world, the general wind direction is constant and known; this is called the prevailing wind, and although it may vary slightly from time to time, it is a good indicator of direction and can help you to navigate. These winds are most effective when there are few or no obstacles to cause the wind's course to be altered – such as mountains, hills, or valleys. Wind blowing across flat areas of desert and the oceans of the world can often be used by sailing craft to navigate great distances.

Trade winds blow very steadily over the oceans and deserts in the areas of the tropics; they vary with the time of the year, but predominately blow towards the doldrums (the area near the Equator that experiences very little wind). In the Northern Hemisphere they blow from the north-east, and in the Southern Hemisphere from the south-east.

Winds that come from a constant direction often indicate the way to the coast. Looking at the way in which the vegetation and plant life are growing can also give a good indication of which direction the sea is in.

Natural indicators
- Prevailing winds cause plants and trees to grow leaning away from them.
- Forests and other dense, tall plant life have shorter growth on the windward side
- Sand dunes have a gentler slope on the windward side

- A build-up of sand and other debris behind plant life indicates the direction from which the wind usually comes.

NATURAL INDICATORS

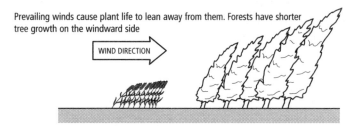

Prevailing winds cause plant life to lean away from them. Forests have shorter tree growth on the windward side

WIND DIRECTION

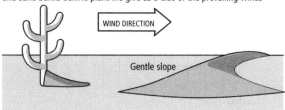

Sand dunes and sand banks behind plant life give us a clue of the prevailing winds

WIND DIRECTION

Gentle slope

There are many natural indicators to help you to determine direction. However, do not rely on just one; use as many as you can to help you to determine the correct direction as accurately as possible.

16. Search and Rescue

The chances are that other people are aware of your situation and will have alerted the authorities, who will initiate a search-and-rescue operation. The type of search depends on the area in which you are marooned, the distances involved and the rescue equipment required for your particular problem.

In most instances where you are stranded because of an aircraft- or ship-related accident, the crew will have transmitted the nature of the problem and the location prior to the incident. Even if they have not been able to notify anyone, the aircraft or ship will be fitted with emergency electronic beacons that are satellite linked, and which will direct the searchers to your exact location. Where this is the case, your task is to stay alive until rescuers arrive, which should not be too long; the best course of action is to stay with the wreckage or as near to it as possible.

If you were travelling in a large vessel or aircraft, the chances are that your exact position will not be known. In these circumstances, the authorities will probably know your general whereabouts, and will send out a search aircraft to pinpoint your exact position before sending out a specific rescue craft or ground search party.

Rescuers in a search aircraft will search in a definite pattern (see below) to ensure that they have covered the area properly.

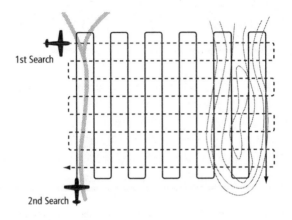

A search aircraft will keep a very tight search pattern, and once it has passed overhead, it will go over again in a crossover direction on the second run.

Where aircraft are not used, teams of experienced searchers carry out the search, and may also bring specially trained dogs with them. There are several recognized ground search methods; the sweep search is the most usual, but it can only be used in circumstances where the terrain is fairly flat with low vegetation. The team members search in line-abreast up to 20m (21.5 yards) apart, keeping visual contact with each other; this distance may be a lot less in poor visibility. The team stands to the right of the lead searcher. After an agreed distance of 100m (107 yards) or so the team stops, usually signalled by one blast of a whistle. The leader turns around on the spot and the rest of the team again take up their positions on his right, and the whole groups set off again. At the end of that search, the leader lines up at the far end of the search line and the whole movement starts again, signalled by two whistles.

Self-rescue

If there is little chance of you being seen from the air or of a rescue attempt being launched, you may be forced to attempt a self-rescue. This should only be decided on as a last resort – and even then with a great deal of thought and planning.

One of the main considerations has to be the best way of travelling. You may decide to build a raft or some other floating craft, and attempt to sail or paddle it in the hope of finding civilization. If you or one of the surviving party know a great deal about navigating rivers, lakes and the sea, and you feel confident that the trip can be successful, then you should think seriously about it. Unfortunately, it is very difficult to build in escape routes in these situations: the flow of a river can change rapidly and without warning, sweeping anything that floats out of control and even over a waterfall; likewise, the sea and large lakes can be hit with high winds that can cause huge waves that can easily overturn a small boat or raft. However, this does not mean that you should not try: if you have looked at all the alternatives, and sailing is your decision, get on with it!

Often it is better to walk out of a survival situation – everyone who is fit and fairly healthy knows how to walk. No matter where we walk, the principles are the same and the dangers pretty obvious.

You may have made the decision to effect a self-rescue on foot because the local terrain is easy to walk in; however, difficult terrain can be encountered at any time, anywhere and at all heights. The problem is that in remote areas you are more likely to encounter difficulties in walking more often and for longer periods. You may not be able to make ample provision when embarking on your walk to safety, so you will need to be extra-careful and vigilant throughout.

Negotiating extensive areas of snow and ice, moorland, scree slopes or dense vegetation not only takes a great deal of time but also requires a great deal of energy. Food is the producer of energy, and therefore you must either have sufficient rations for the 'walkout' or have the confidence and ability to procure your food as you go. When lying in your shelter, eating a handful of berries or a teaspoon of honey will give your body a boost of energy lasting from 30 minutes to an hour; on a trek, that same energy will be burnt up in half a minute. You can help to conserve energy if you take time to plan your route. It is not always the best policy to take what looks like the shortest route to an objective; quite often, a longer, simpler route will be quicker or safer and less tiring.

Good route-planning prior to your walk will at best alleviate the necessity to walk through hazards, and at worst will give you prior warning; this is obviously easier if you have maps or charts – if not, take the high ground and see if you can pick out a decent route. Map or not, note down the route breaking the walk into small sections and study each one, noting potential problems and prominent features that can be seen from everywhere. If possible, identify any obvious linear features such as rivers or the edge of mountain ranges.

Try to keep the route at a constant height – doing this will help to conserve energy and help the less-experienced members to feel more confident. Ascending and descending for no apparent reason will quickly demoralize even the hardiest and most experienced of walkers. Where it is necessary to fluctuate in height, choose slopes that are gradual and, if possible, scenic as these will make the effort more rewarding.

You must plan to end the day's trek well before nightfall in as safe an area as possible, with enough time for everyone to make an overnight shelter and prepare a meal. It will help if you have already studied and noted the local times of dusk and dawn.

Estimating time to distance is an important skill that must be mastered by everyone who is 'walking out'. The following rule of thumb will assist, although it must be remembered that individuals have differing levels of pace and stamina, and in certain locations such as the jungle you will be very lucky to achieve a kilometre (½ a mile) a day – nevertheless, the rules are there as a guide and can be altered to suit:

Carrying a light pack, estimate:	Carrying a full pack estimate:
12 minutes per kilometre, + 1 minute for every 10 metres ascended	15 minutes per kilometre + 1 minute per 10 metres ascended
On a map scale of 1:50,000, 1 cm = 6 minutes; and one contour is 10 metres (1 minute)	On a map scale of 1:50,000, 1 cm = 7 minutes; and one contour is 10 metres (1 minute)
On a map scale of 1:25,000, 1 cm = 3 minutes; and one contour is 5 metres (30 seconds).	On a map scale of 1:25,000, 1 cm = 4 minutes; and one contour is 5 metres (30 seconds)

Although you may have made a plan of the route you intend to take, you may have to alter this during the course of the day, but this should be done only in the most extreme circumstances. If the decision has been made, you must indicate the change from the agreed route by leaving a definite mark using one of the recognized trail-blazing signs. If you do this, a following search party that has been made aware of your proposed route (perhaps by documentary evidence left at the crash site, or from information given from other survivors you left behind or were lost and then found) can easily follow your detours.

TRAIL BLAZING

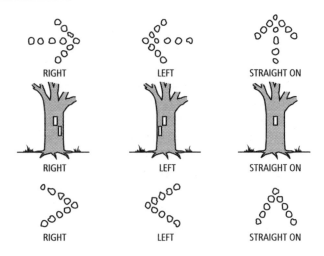

If you have decided to walk to safety. you must leave an easily followed route.

Before the self-rescue walkout, and during its course, everyone involved should know the exact purpose, the route to be taken, the aims and objectives, timings, expected difficulties and the reason behind any diversions or detours. For the sake of keeping a sense of teamwork and morale, it is better if a leader is appointed; a second person should also be appointed to take control if needed. Both of these people should ideally be experienced in navigation and walking, although if they are not then they should have leadership qualities – not least confidence and a sense of humour. Throughout, these key members must keep each other fully aware of the situation and the feelings of the rest of the group.

The briefing of the whole group can be done well in advance of the actual walkout, and any problems can be ironed out in plenty of time. Once the route is decided, all members can be given full details. Everyone involved – including those who you are leaving behind, or who are walking out by a different route – should have full knowledge of the task and, if possible, a written route plan (if they are later found dead, they won't be able to give the information verbally).

At the pre-walkout briefing, the leader's responsibility will be to give full details of the number of people involved in the walk, and information about those left behind and any that are taking another route. Any equipment, clothing, food and water should be distributed fairly, based on the likelihood of any of the groups being able to support themselves. Overall safety and the procedures to follow in the event of an accident – including recognized and agreed distress signalling – should also be agreed. If flares are available, then these should be distributed between the groups that are most likely to be in a position to discharge them. For example, if one group is moving through dense jungle or forests, and another group has been left at the crash site in open ground, then the majority of the flares should remain with them.

There will always be mixed abilities in all groups, and this has to be accounted for when planning a self-rescue attempt. It is important for the leader to recognize this fact and draw attention to it during the early stages of the briefing; any members who may be daunted by the task need to be reassured early on.

Clothing and equipment should be decided on as soon as possible. In fact, if you do not have any appropriate clothing and equipment, then you may decide not to take the chance of walking out at all. If you do decide to go ahead, then it is worth using all the combined resources and apportioning the best equipment to the walkers. Any members of the group you leave behind probably do not need the toughest footwear, or water- and windproof clothing – especially if they have well-established shelters and fires. If you expect to be walking over deep, soft snow, you may have to make snow-shoes, which can be made from wreckage or by using young supple shoots from trees or other vegetation. You may be fortunate enough to have ropes with you, or you can strip electric wiring from vehicle wreckage to use as ropes. If not, try stripping down vehicle interiors and cutting any material into long, thin strips, and then either tie them together or plait them to make a safety rope.

Having gathered together your clothing, equipment, food, water and anything else you need, you will have to carry it all. Once again, you can turn to the wreckage and any luggage on site, or resort to making a carrier from any natural materials you can find. Packs should be strapped to your back with the weight held on your hips – the higher the pack sits, the better. Make sure that you pack your equipment and clothing in such a way that you can take out regularly used items such as protective clothing easily.

Once the self-rescue walkout begins, it is up to every member to watch out for each other. If you are on your own, then you should take extra care, making absolutely sure that you do not put yourself in danger. Getting lost is not a rare occurrence in these situations, but the more experience you have, the less it happens. Once you realize that you are lost, retrace your steps until you come back to a place you remember, and then try again. As a leader of a group, do not try to bluff: if you are lost, say you are – even the most inexperienced group will know when something is wrong, and a competent leader will always be honest and admit the problem. The test of leadership will be decided by how well the leader reacts and how confident he is.

When there is a problem, a group discussion is the best way of approaching it and deciding on appropriate action: on no account should the group split up. This action is the type that makes a difficult situation into a dangerous one. Once a decision has been made, it needs to be carried through with confidence.

When you are hopelessly lost, the best course of action is to head for a linear feature. By doing this, the group simply moves in the general direction of the linear feature, and sooner or later they will come across it. Once you have reached it, it will be much easier to decide in which direction to proceed as there will be only two to choose from.

Throughout the trek, make a mental note of any prominent features you pass – especially the ones that were noted/identified at the planning stage (making a simple sketch of the area during planning is useful). As the group moves along the route, they should be encouraged to look around – especially behind them. If anything goes wrong, they can use this visual knowledge to find their way back. If you are fortunate enough to have a compass with you, you should be constantly taking bearings to and from known features (see the *Map and Compass* section): poor visibility can happen in a matter of minutes as the weather and surroundings change.

When poor visibility does hamper navigation, or when you are forced to move over featureless terrain, the group may have to rely on a compass, the stars, or the sun alone; this is achieved by three or more of the group working together. One member stands still using the compass to line up his colleagues, one in front of the other – the last walking as far forward as possible – in sight of the rear man; the group moves along in this leap-frog-type manoeuvre until the situation changes.

BLIND ROUTE FINDING

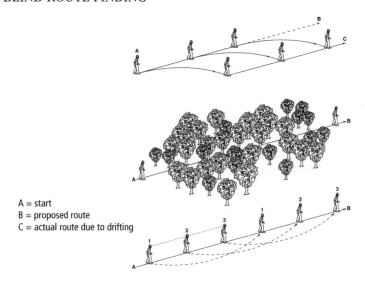

A = start
B = proposed route
C = actual route due to drifting

In featureless terrain or poor visibility, being able to keep to your planned route will depend on team work. Beware of the effect of drifting off course. Line up before you move.

When sighting a distant feature, it is worth using one that is not too far away. In hot climates, heat rising from the ground distorts the view, and consequently bearings taken cannot be relied on. The same can be said for bearings that have been taken near to large underground pipe works (which are often found in the desert), magnetic rocks or during magnetic storms. The latter are undetectable until they happen, whereas the former are marked on good-quality charts and maps.

When the walkout group first sets off, there will be a tendency to force the pace: this must be avoided. A steady, rhythmic pace taken from the group's slowest member is best. A group that is out of breath soon tires, with the weaker members feeling the strain first and then dropping back. In this position they soon become disheartened, and group morale suffers.

It will probably be necessary from time to time to negotiate rock outcrops, especially when you are moving at higher altitudes and are having to negotiate peaks. Inexperienced people often put a spurt on to reach the top, but what looks like the top rarely is the actual peak – more often than not there are a number of false peaks that can quickly sap energy and undermine morale. As has already been pointed out, wherever possible you should aim to get down off the peaks, but this is not always easy to do, and if you are relying on being spotted from the air it may actually prevent you from being seen.

When rock outcrops confront you, your only course may be to climb. In this case, a rope should ideally be available to protect the group, but it should not be used for climbing – it is there to give the climber confidence and to arrest a fall. Where climbing belts are not available, the climbers should be tied on – preferably with a single bowline knot (under no circumstances should you use ordinary clothing belts). The safety rope should be secured and controlled by a competent member of the group, who is in turn secured by means of a belay. The principle with the belay is that one member climbs and is attached by the rope, which is held by the belayer. He in turn is attached by a loop of rope to a secure anchor point directly behind him and in line with the climber.

Very steep slopes are best negotiated by abseiling, although this should be the last resort and should not be attempted without adequate ropes.

The classic abseil technique

Abseiling is a method of descent that involves the climber sliding down the rope and using friction to control the rate of descent. The rope is used doubled and looped around an abseil point, which may be a rock, tree or some other secure feature – ensure that you have tied the two loose ends of the rope together to form a continual loop. In snow and ice, you may have to cut a snow bollard; this takes a lot of time, but may well be the only way in which you can secure the rope well enough to use for abseiling or belay protection. The bollard is a mushroom shape cut deep in the snow. The stork must be at least 1.5m (4 ½ft) thick and 0.5m (18ins) deep; the rope is passed around this and must be protected from cutting into the snow by arranging packs or spare clothing between the rope and snow to form a friction guard (be sure to attach these items to the main rope). When the last climber is down, the rope is then pulled through, along with the important items you have used as a friction guard.

There are several devices on the market that are manufactured to assist in the abseil technique. You may be fortunate enough to have some of this equipment with you, but if not, then you will have to use the classic abseil method.

Having secured the rope and tied the loose ends together, you must check that it reaches the ground, or some safe rest area below your position, and that it is not caught or twisted. Stand astride the rope facing the anchor, and take the rope in front of you in the left hand and the rope behind you in the right hand. Holding it both in front and behind your body, pull it up so that it touches the underside of your inside right thigh. Pass it around the right leg and diagonally across the chest and over the left shoulder; let go with the right hand and use it to grip the free hanging ropes behind you. The technique now is to move backwards a little at a time with the body turned slightly to the right and leading with the right leg, allowing the rope to slide around the body. To stop, simply move the right hand and rope to the front of the body – the extra friction will halt the descent.

The classic abseil is uncomfortable, and if you are forced to use it a lot then you should put some padding between the rope and the thigh; taking your time and keeping your back straight will help. Avoid being forced to bend forward, as on a long abseil this position can make breathing difficult. Two other methods – the sling and karabiner, and using a piece of specifically designed abseil equipment such as the Figure of Eight Descendeur – make the technique a lot easier and less painful. However, they both need specific equipment, which may not be available.

Abseiling can also be used as a method of escape from situations such as burning buildings and aircraft (see the *Terrorism – Hostage* section).

Because friction is the braking force of the abseil, great care must be taken to ensure that the age and type of rope used can withstand the strain. Many experienced mountaineers have lost their lives in abseiling accidents, and the following list records some of the causes:

- Anchor points not secure and ropes riding off
- Descent too fast, burning hands when trying to slow down
- Clothing and hair trapped

- Rope too short for the next safe stance
- Rope chopped by falling stone
- Abseiler knocked unconscious by falling stone
- Rope jammed around the anchor, stopping it from being retrieved
- Rope jams after clearing anchor and abseiler climbs back up and dislodges the hung rope
- Abseiler throws two ends of the rope over the cliff, but forgets to tie off
- Abseiler rests on a ledge part way down the abseil; as he releases his weight; the elasticity of the rope causes a ripple to run up and flicks the rope off its anchor.

ABSEILING

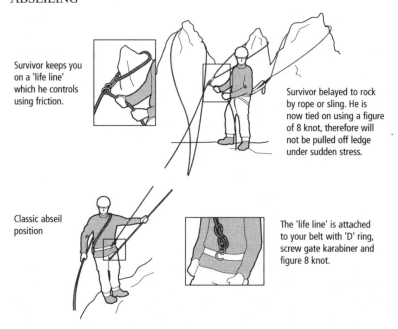

Survivor keeps you on a 'life line' which he controls using friction.

Survivor belayed to rock by rope or sling. He is now tied on using a figure of 8 knot, therefore will not be pulled off ledge under sudden stress.

Classic abseil position

The 'life line' is attached to your belt with 'D' ring, screw gate karabiner and figure 8 knot.

Before you decide to use abseil techniques, make sure that your equipment is adequate for the task.

As the trek progresses, there will be a need for the group to take rest periods; these must be of short duration to avoid the possibility of becoming stiff and cold. As soon as the group stops walking, they should put on warm clothing if it's available, cuddle up together to share body heat and take shelter from the wind. Any injuries that have developed need to be looked at. For example, if footwear is too tight, adjusting socks will probably avoid the development of blisters. Any hot spots need to be protected, which can be done by smearing the area with animal fat, or simply massaging the area and adjusting footwear. Usually five to ten minutes in every hour will be sufficient for members of the group to sort themselves out. Plenty of liquids need to be taken, and small amounts of food regularly taken will improve overall stamina and morale. If food and water are scarce, keep the pace and distance down until you have the opportunity to replenish both.

Areas of soft ground, dense vegetation, scree, rocks, gullies and damp slippery places are best avoided. Not only are they dangerous, but they slow the pace down considerably. Where possible, keep to animal tracks, but be aware that the animals may not take too kindly to you using them.

In mountainous areas, if you cannot get lower down, use the ridges to avoid the tiring effect of walking on the side of the hill. When moving in remote areas where there are no paths, ascend and descend in single file, and if there is the likelihood of dislodging loose rocks, move in line-abreast. On very steep, loose slopes, use a zigzag pattern – keeping the group close together so that if rocks are dislodged, they do not have the distance to gather enough speed to make them dangerous. Where this is impossible, move the group in small sections, halting on safe ground while those below follow. Regardless of the position of the group, always assume that there is someone lower down, and shout, 'Below!' as loudly as possible when anything is dislodged. You should also do this when you are static and surviving in a mountain area; it would be disastrous if you inadvertently caused a rock fall on top of an ascending rescue team.

Well packed, short grass is by far the easiest ground to walk on, but it can be dangerous when it is present on exposed hillsides and prone to a layer of ground frost. When wet, the grass becomes very slippery, and walkers wearing waterproofs have no resistance if they stumble and fall. Descents are quicker on grass slopes, but a direct route must only be taken if there is a continual view to lower ground. High grass and bracken make walking difficult and slow: it is better to find a route around this type of ground.

When climbing, grass, bracken and small shrubs should not be used as hand-holds; these plants are usually shallow-rooted, and bracken in particular can cause severe cuts to your hands if your grip fails.

Heather is difficult to walk through: it grows in thick clumps that merge into one another and often cover deep fissures; caution is needed, as there is a risk of falling through.

Scree can provide a pleasant descent if you know how to walk on it, but it can lead to accidents, as the small broken rocks are often balanced precariously and can shift without warning. Large scree is best avoided as it takes a lot of energy to climb over, and the constant shift of balance causes lower limb injuries.

Large areas of soft, wet ground are normal in moorland areas. Such ground is rarely dangerous, but it is best avoided as it is difficult to move in, and the constant wet may cause trench foot (see *Medical* section).

At some time or other, streams, river and lakes will have to be negotiated. However, they should be circumnavigated where possible, or crossed by bridge – even if it means that extra time is added to the journey (see the *Surviving Water* section).

Be Weather-Wise

If you have taken the decision to walk out to safety, or you have made up your mind to paddle or sail, you need to consider the weather that you may experience. In all outdoor survival situations, the weather will play a big part in your decision-making process. In many regions, such as sand deserts, tropical jungles, the Arctic and Antarctica, weather patterns are very predictable, but in other regions the weather can be very changeable. Being able to read the weather will help you to make decisions about self-rescue and overall protection.

Cloud formations are a very reliable indicator of developing weather. The height of the cloud formation is important in determining the likelihood of rain and the amount that will fall. Very high clouds are known as *cirrus*, and appear as delicate wisps of white cloud; these are associated with fine weather. Once they begin to become feathery, they are often referred to as 'mare's tales'; this is due to winds blowing at high altitudes, and is a sign of strong winds at ground level later. *Cirrocumulus* clouds are arranged in lines across the sky, and resemble the lines found on mackerel – many sailors and outdoor people refer to this as a 'mackerel sky', and it is a sign that the current fine weather is on its way out. The clouds merge, forming a white sheet of cloud known as *cirrostratus*, in which there is a halo effect around the sun and moon; rain at this stage is not usually heavy, and soon passes. Once the mackerel cloud thickens, it forms medium-height clouds known as *altocumulus*, characteristically seen as large, rounded clouds slightly grey in colour and in lines. These join together, forming a watery grey sheet – the sun may be seen through a blue hazy veil. This type of formation indicates a warm front coming through; these fronts can be up to 250 kilometres (166 miles) long and move at 19mph (30 kph), and the resulting rain can last for ten hours or more. Low cloud is known as *stratocumulus*, typically seen as huge lumpy masses over the whole sky; It is particularly formed in cold climates, and often has a wavy top lit by the sun. Afterwards, they can form a dark blanket of *stratus*, which can develop into *nimbostratus* – heavy dark clouds with no form to them and ragged edges. These are true rain clouds, and will definitely let loose their water.

Cumulus clouds have great vertical structures, seen as thick white clouds several miles deep with a horizontal base and billowing top. These are fine-weather clouds, but may develop into threatening thunderstorm clouds shaped like an anvil, known as *cumulonimbus*.

The above cloud types are seen in temperate regions; at the poles, the cloud formations are much lower, whereas they appear higher in the tropics.

The moon and stars can also give a clue to imminent weather changes. When the moon shines weakly through a haze, it is an indication of approaching rain; a clear, bright moon in winter conditions is a sign of heavy frost; while when the moon has a reddish tint it is a sign of an approaching wind.

A red sky at night is a very good indication that the following day will be a good, calm day without rain, but if there is a red sky in the early morning, a wet period on its way.

17. Attracting Attention

Whether you have stayed in one location or have decided that your chances of survival would be better if you moved out, you should always be ready to make your position known. There is documented evidence to show that some survivors did not have their signalling equipment available when a potential rescuer was nearby. As a result, they missed an early rescue opportunity, and had to survive for many months before another chance came their way.

Always make sure that you are ready to attract attention to yourself and your situation from the moment you realize you are in trouble.

If there is vehicle wreckage, then spread it around in open country so that it can be seen from the air. Shiny metal panels and bright materials should be placed on high ground in a position that catches the sun and reflects the light. In areas where you are hidden from sight because of a thick canopy of vegetation, climb up above the canopy and spread bright clothing and other materials on top of the trees. Try constructing a simple kite, and keep it flying.

If there is a river or stream, make a small raft, build a signal fire on it and float it downstream; this is especially effective at night. Even if the fire goes out, it will attract the interest of local tribes if found by them.

In dense vegetation, the noise of approaching aircraft or other vehicles is deadened. If you are not prepared, you may not have time to signal; therefore keep all of your signalling devices close at hand at all times.

If you have the resources, keep a fire going. During the day, flames cannot be seen, but making the fire very smoky by burning fresh green leaves or engine oil will create a good signal. During darkness, smoke cannot be seen, so you should change your approach and create clean, bright flames by burning petrol, aviation fuel or very dry wood.

If you consider that other human beings may be in the area, you can shout; this is more effective if you make shouting a group activity, and shouting down-wind will help to carry your voices further. Where there is a large amount of plant and tree life, your voice will not carry very far, so in these situations you will have a greater chance of being heard if you use wooden drum-sticks to rhythmically beat a tree trunk – particularly if the tree is dead and hollow.

18. International Distress Signalling

Throughout the world, there are agreed protocols for officially signalling distress. Although in many areas you would still get a response if you used some of the methods outlined in the *Attracting Attention* section, these may be misunderstood, whereas with the agreed international distress signals action will be taken without delay.

The protocol sets out a series of visual and audible signals or a mixture of both to communicate that there is a serious risk to life.

Whenever you or your family members are travelling away from home, you should carry a whistle and a torch with you. Neither of these needs to be large. With these two simple additions, you have the ability to carry out international distress signalling.

Any time you are out and about you are at risk, and a simple miscalculation or accident is potentially sufficient of an emergency for you to have to summon help; you do not have to be miles from civilization before the need arises. There have been many occasions on which a vehicle has left a main highway and overturned down an embankment out of sight of passing motorists. With the occupants unable to get out, a whistle could easily have been used to attract attention.

Whenever you feel that you are in distress, or approaching danger, you should consider using the recognized international distress signals listed below. Only you can decide whether or not assistance is really needed. If you are not sure, ask yourself these two simple questions:

1. What are the implications if I do use a distress signal?
2. What are the consequences if I don't?

The main implication may be loss of face if it was inappropriately used, but the consequence may be loss of life if you didn't signal at all!

INTERNATIONAL DISTRESS SIGNALS

Message	Pyrotechnic	Audible	Visual
I want help	1 red or succession of reds (A)	Mountain distress signal (C) or SOS whistle (C)	Pyro signal Mountain distress signal SOS (lightly) (C)
Message understood (B)	1 white or succession of whites used by party on the hill (A)	Mountain distress (D)	Mountain distress (D)
Position of base camp	1 white or yellow or a succession of whites or yellows	No audible signal to be used	Steady white in yellow light(s) (car head spot or search lights pointed upwards if possible)
Recall to base camp	A succession of greens	A succession of thunder-flashes, notes on horn, bell, whistle etc	A succession of white or yellow light(s) swtiched on and off (or a long-burning flare).

A. Thunder-flashes should be used to attract attention before signalling.

B. message understood. It is not always advisable to send a reply or to make the 'Message understood' code. It may cause those in distress to stop signalling before their position is accurately fixed.

C. Mountain distress signal. Six long calls, flashes, whistles, etc, in quick succession, repeated at one-minute intervals.

D. Mountain distress reply. Three long calls, flashes, whistles, etc, in quick succession, repeated at one-minute intervals.

E. SOS. Three short, three long and three short calls, flashes, whistles etc (...---...)

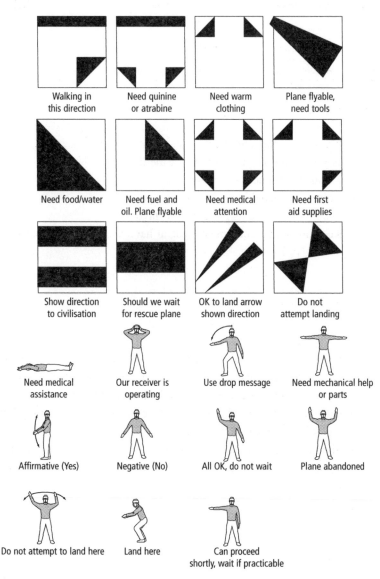

Walking in this direction	Need quinine or atrabine	Need warm clothing	Plane flyable, need tools
Need food/water	Need fuel and oil. Plane flyable	Need medical attention	Need first aid supplies
Show direction to civilisation	Should we wait for rescue plane	OK to land arrow shown direction	Do not attempt landing
Need medical assistance	Our receiver is operating	Use drop message	Need mechanical help or parts
Affirmative (Yes)	Negative (No)	All OK, do not wait	Plane abandoned
Do not attempt to land here	Land here	Can proceed shortly, wait if practicable	

Message	Code Symbol	Message	Code Symbol
Require doctor, serious injuries	I	Will attempt take off	▷
Require medical supplies	I I	Aircraft seriously damaged	⊡
Unable to proceed	X	Probably safe to land here	△
Require food and water	F	Require fuel and oil	⅃
Require firearms and ammunition	⋙	All well	LL
Require map and compass	☐	No	N
Require signal lamp, battery, radio	⁝	Yes	Y
Indicate direction to proceed	K	Not understood	⅃L
Am proceeding in this direction	↑	Require engineer	W

Signalling tips

- If you are using a torch or vehicle lights to signal, use a shield such as your hand or a jacket to mask the light; switching lights on and off quickly reduces the battery life
- Noise is carried down-wind; where appropriate, turn with your back to the wind to use its force in your favour
- Keep signalling equipment close at hand at all times so that it can be used quickly
- If you are using flares or other pyrotechnic devices. make sure there is nothing above you that they can hit or be caught on
- When you are using ground-to-air signals, make them as large and clear as possible; you can make them boldly in the snow or sand using the shadows to enhance them
- Using Morse Code to signal SOS (... --- ...) may seem like a good idea, but if it is answered in Morse can you read it? If not, and you do not respond, the rescuers may think it is a hoax call
- Once you have made contact with rescuers, keep signalling until you know they can actually see you
- Should you ever use a signal, and then for any reason move from the signal site, make sure you trail blaze (see *the Search and Rescue* section)
- If you have signalled and then manage to effect a self-rescue, tell the authorities so that they can call off any search-and-rescue operation they may have put in progress.

PART 4
Water

19. The Body's Needs

In the civilized world, water is taken for granted by the vast majority of people; a great deal of water is wasted simply because there is an abundance of it, and little thought is given to the reliance of human life on water. The human body requires a certain amount of fluid to maintain its everyday functions; without sufficient water, the body soon becomes inefficient. Exhaustion caused by dehydration results in further dehydration and eventual kidney failure, with death occurring soon afterwards. Once the kidneys fail, there is no way of sustaining life in a survival situation – even with expert medical assistance and hospitalization, there is little likelihood of recovery.

For survival, it is vital that water is taken regularly. It is possible to go without food for 20 or 30 days, but without water you would be lucky to live for six. I was once told that ten days was possible, but in my experience even three days without any water results in serious, adverse effects on the body's metabolism – causing severe headaches and a lack of energy so profound that it becomes very difficult to motivate oneself enough to find a source. Even in temperate climates you need to drink a minimum of one-and-a-half litres (3pints) of water in a 24-hour period to maintain body efficiency, and in hot climates this increases to a minimum of six litres (12 pints). However, it is possible to live for a limited period on as little as 250 ml (half a pint). To do this, you have to conserve your body's fluid level by reducing sweating – which means sleeping and resting as much as possible during the day, especially in hot climates. Breathing through your nose and keeping your mouth closed also reduces the amount of water vapour the body will lose. Taking care of your personal hygiene and ensuring clean food preparation can help you to avoid sickness and diarrhoea – the biggest causes of body fluid loss in a survival situation. If you smoke, this will contribute to dehydration, so you should stop smoking or at least smoke as little as possible when drinking water is short. Drinking alcohol also dehydrates the body, so this should definitely be avoided in a survival situation. In fact, any alcoholic drinks should be emptied into shallow containers and placed into a solar still to extract the water content (see later section); the resulting alcohol can then be used for medical applications. Water is also needed to help with the digestion of food, so cutting back on food intake will help to maintain body fluid levels. When you do eat, there are two rules you should keep in mind:

1. Foods high in carbohydrates, such as sugars and starches, require only a minimum amount of water for digestion.
2. Protein foods such as meat, fish, eggs and especially seaweed, require large amounts of water for digestion, and should be avoided until there is sufficient water available.

Although we often feel thirsty, this is not a good indicator of the body's true need for water. Consequently you should not drink just because you feel thirsty – monitoring your water intake is a far better way of keeping control. You can allay the feeling of thirst by sucking a button, pebble or other similar object.

Do not drink sea water: the high salt content will only make matters worse. However, you can extract water from it with the use of a solar still in the same way as you can extract the water from alcoholic drinks; the resulting salt crystals left in the container can be kept and used in cooking and food preparation, or heavily diluted to help to maintain the body's balance of salt. Drinking urine may seem like a good idea, but in fact urine is one of the ways in which the body transports waste products out of the system; reintroducing them back into the body will cause you to become ill and lead to kidney failure. Instead, keep the urine and use the solar-still method to extract the pure water.

If you do not have any containers, the foul water can be emptied on the ground under the still, or soaked up in a cloth and placed inside.

If you are relying solely on a solar still, then you will have to ration the water, but rationing should only be introduced in the most extreme circumstances. There are a number of different rationing theories, but the one I favour is the following:

WATER RATIONING SCHEDULE
Day one: no water is issued except for the injured.

Days two, three and four: 400 ml (⅔ pint) issued per person.
Day five onwards: 100–300 ml (½ pint) issued daily per person.

This system is by no means ideal, but at least it will maximize your chances of survival.

If you can maintain the following water intake, you should not have any problems:

Degrees Celcius	Litres per 24 hours
25°	1.0 (2 pints)
30°	2.0 (4 pints)
35°	5.0–6.0 (10-12 pints)

20. The solar still

In areas where there is little rainfall, you may have to resort to the use of a solar still. This is by no means the perfect solution, but it does work if constructed correctly. The solar-still principle works by interrupting the normal cycle of water vapour as it rises from the ground on its way to forming clouds, which causes the water to condense onto a surface. When sufficient condensation is gathered, it can then be collected into a container and stored ready for drinking.

This method was first developed by Dr Ray D. Jackson and Dr Cornelius van Bavel, who both worked for the United States water conservation authority. The idea came from First World War soldiers, who often slept under their rubberized gas capes; in the mornings, it was noted that the underside of these capes was covered in water droplets. Realizing that this was condensed water vapour that had come from the soldiers' bodies, the two doctors developed an idea for using the principle to produce water in arid regions. They carried out experiments in several desert locations using different equipment designs, and recorded their findings. The solar-still design described here proved to be the most effective: even in the hottest and driest deserts, they recorded a minimum of one pint of water collected in a 24-hour period.

However, having tried this method in a number of hot, dry locations, I have never managed to collect a pint or anywhere near that amount of water. A former British military survival and tracking expert I once knew agreed that the solar still can be a life-saving piece of equipment, but it needs careful siting, construction and help to speed up the production cycle.

The basic small still begins with a round hole, which should be approximately 60–70cm (2ft) deep and 1.5m (4 ½ft) wide; a receptacle should be placed in the bottom-centre of the hole. It helps if you have a tube or straw long enough to reach from the bottom of the receptacle to the outer edge of the hole – although this isn't essential, it allows you to extract the water without constantly disturbing the still. Once the hole has been dug and the container and straw placed inside, stretch a piece of polythene, canvas or other waterproof material over the hole, sealing it with a mound of earth around its circumference. Place a stone or other heavy object in the centre of the sheet, causing it to sag in the centre and making a conical shape (it is possible to use a piece of thin metal such as a vehicle panel, although it could take a great deal of effort to work the material into shape if you don't have suitable tools to hand).

The still is operated by the sun's heat raising the temperature of the air and sand/soil under the sheeting, thus hastening the evaporation of any water held in the ground. It will help if you place green vegetation in the bottom of the hole; you can also urinate in there, or pour in foul water from vehicle radiators, or put in salt water, or empty the urine from the bladders of any animals you may have killed for food. Once the evaporation process begins, the vapour precipitates and the water droplets cling to the underside of the material, eventually running down the slope and dripping into the receptacle you have placed in there. You will collect more water if the underside of the material is as rough as possible.

Natural water and sea water distilled and collected in this way, direct from the ground, needs no purification and is safe to drink. Water that is gathered by the evaporation process using urine and other foul water should be purified following collection by one of the methods described below.

THE SOLAR STILL

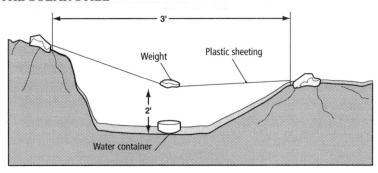

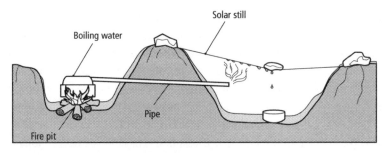

The solar still is a life-saving water provider. It should be constructed with care and sited in a location where water vapour is naturally stored.

If the still is constructed in dry river beds, in areas where there is bed rock or in natural depressions, there is a better chance of a good supply of water.

You should not rely on one still: the more you construct, the better your chances will be of collecting sufficient water to live on.

You can consider making an addition to the basic solar still, involving the digging of a second hole next to the solar still where a fire can be lit. On this fire you can place a kettle of foul water and run a pipe from the spout through the wall of the fire pit and into the still. The resulting steam will condense in the normal way, and greatly add to your water production. If you do not have a conventional kettle, manufacture one using vehicle and other wreckage parts, or use large bamboo as the pot with small bamboo side-shoots as the pipe. Keeping the fire burning very low will regulate the steam, giving it a chance to condense rather than filling the still, and expanding the life of the boiling apparatus.

21. Purifying

Never assume that water is safe to drink: unless you know the source and you are certain of its cleanliness, take no chances. If you have any doubt at all about the quality of the water, purify it using one of the recognized methods described below. The fact that water looks clean is no indication of its true state.

Purification methods

Many outdoor and travel shops sell filter straws that clean the water as it passes through the straw; these do not cost a lot of money, and are worth adding to your first-aid kit or travel bag. Halazone tablets can also be purchased and are excellent for cleansing water, although they can be dangerous if you don't use them according to the instructions.

If you do not have purpose-made chemical cleansers, you will have to resort to boiling the water to kill harmful bacteria. Many people believe that boiling water for three minutes is sufficient in order to purify it, but you boil eggs for three minutes! To purify water effectively, it must be boiled for at least 15 minutes, but if this is impracticable, use the solar-still principle to clean the water.

22. Locating

Keep a weather-eye on the sky: you should be able to tell when rain or snow is on the way (see the *Weather-wise* section). All rainwater and snow is safe to drink – as long as poisons from things such as dangerous vegetation, or bacteria found in dirty containers and collecting equipment, have not contaminated it. Throughout your survival fight, have as many water-collecting containers available as possible ready to catch the rain: you cannot have too much fresh water. If you are using solar stills, then these will act as rainwater collection points, but they will need emptying throughout the downpour in order to stop the additional weight collapsing them. When rain does come, if you do not have any suitable or empty water containers available, use clothing and material to act as sponges to soak up the water; you can either suck the water from the clothing or wring it out to top up your water supplies.

All green vegetation needs water to live. A plant's root system draws water from the soil, transports it through the stem and delivers it to the leaves, where it assists in the production of food. Not all the water is used in this process, and the excess leaves the plant in vapour form. If you consider how huge trees can be and how many leaves are involved, you can see that hundreds of litres of water evaporate daily. Although it's impracticable to seal each leaf of a tree with a polythene bag, if you did so your water-supply problems would be over.

In a survival situation you have to adapt yourself to the environment. Thinking laterally and using common sense could help you to turn a problem into a life-saving advantage. For example, using your knowledge of the plant cycle explained above, you could cut a 'V' shape into the tree and collect the sap as it rises, in the same way as rubber is tapped; both common birch and aspen can be tapped in this way and the watery sap drunk. If you carry out this procedure on other trees that may be unfamiliar to you, put the sap in the solar still and then boil the water in the usual way. Avoid drinking water directly from trees that you do not know are safe; If the sap is milky or very discoloured, assume that it is toxic, and should therefore not be used or handled. As I have stated earlier, you may not have a supply of polythene bags to cover a tree, but if you have any wreckage at your disposal – especially aircraft wreckage – there may be a supply of the thin rubber gloves used by the cabin crew; these can be attached to vegetation and will soon be collecting water for you. Even a light waterproof jacket or any other waterproof material will cover with dew if you lay it on grass or over dense vegetation – turning it over carefully keeps the water in place, and allows you to mop it off or shape the material to use as a funnel to add it to your reservoir.

Many plants have evolved in such a way that they trap water and hold it in their own containers; this water can be collected and purified. In the jungle, many of the vines that hang from the trees carry water that you can drink. The floor-level end of the vine holds most of the reservoir, being full of water up to about a metre in length. Cutting this off without disturbing the base will allow you to drink the cool, fresh water without losing any. Not all vines have water that is safe to drink, however: as with trees, those with milky or very discoloured liquid should be left alone.

Bamboo is another plant which has a good supply of clean water that is easy to access. The water is held between the bamboo segments: cutting into these segments will release the water.

Sea ice over a year old has no noticeable saltiness, the heavier saline particles having sunk to the bottom of the ice slab. Sea ice over three years old is generally fresher than the water in most rivers, while old sea ice can be distinguished by its rounded corners and its bluish tint. Icebergs are similar, although you should take great care if they are in your area; if you stand on one, it may roll over and you may be thrown into the water, and it might even sink your craft.

Snow and ice should be melted to provide fresh water. If you are using a container over a fire, put a little ice and snow in at a time and wait for it to melt fully before adding to it. Do not compress snow in a container and place it on a heat source: the snow will melt a little at the base of the pan, but the rest will not melt quickly enough and the pan bottom will burn through. Do not suck ice or snow either, as it can freeze your mouth, or you could choke if the ice becomes stuck in your throat.

During the summer months, water can be collected from streams, rivers and pools, but do not take water from the edges of these sources as debris often collects there. In winter, you can collect snow and ice. No natural water freezes completely, and you may have more success in breaking the ice and collecting the water from below. A build-up of snow on ice has the effect of insulating the water from the cold: the deeper the snow, the shallower the ice. When collecting water in this way, be very careful that you do not put yourself in danger and fall through the ice.

In areas where you cannot locate a water supply, use animal and insect life in your area to lead you to water. They all need water to live, although, unlike humans, they can drink foul water without coming to any harm. When you find water in this way, make sure you purify it before drinking.

If you see a line of ants or other communal insects, follow it until you find their water source. Birds, especially seed-eating birds, need a lot of water, so watch carefully how they are flying; birds flying fast and low through the trees or vegetation without stopping are probably going toward water, whereas if they are flying from branch to branch they are usually full of water and are coming away from the source. If you can, trap an animal that is unlikely to attack you (without killing it), and tie a long lead around its neck; stake the animal out overnight. The following day release it, making sure that you keep hold of its lead; do not restrict its movements, and let it wander where it wants to. At first, it will attempt to evade you and be distressed, but eventually it will settle down and have to make its way to its watering place. Once the animal has led you to the water, kill it for your next meal.

At the shoreline underground fresh water will meet the heavier saltwater – usually on the landward side of dunes. Dig down until your hole fills with water, then stop digging and allow the water to settle sufficiently to allow the sediment and the salt water to sink to the bottom – which may take several hours. When the water has settled, use your hand or a shallow container to skim the top layer off the water: if the water is salty, dig another hole further away from the shore. Continue doing this until you find fresh water.

All water found in the ground tastes earthy and brackish, even after you have purified it. However, you do get used to the taste eventually.

Filtering

One thing that is certain is that when you are in a survival situation, any water you find will not be as clean and fresh as you are used to. Making a filter will help you to sift out any debris in the water, and there are several ways of doing this. On the seashore, you can pass the water through a container full of broken shells and tiny pebbles, while in other locations using straw or heather as your filter material will suffice; if you have spare clothing or bandages, these can also be used. However, unless there is absolutely no alternative, avoid using woollen clothes – I speak from experience here, and can tell you that although it works the wool taints the water and it tastes awful! No matter how much you filter water using these techniques, you will not remove all the particles in it. No matter how well your filter works, do not assume that the water has been purified: it won't. Use one of the accepted purifying procedures described above before attempting to drink the water or using it to wash anything that you intend to eat, or to wash your mouth or clean your teeth.

Quick water tips

- If you know that water is going to be a problem, make sure that you carry enough for your entire journey
- Where water is stored for emergency use, such as in lifeboats, check and change it regularly
- Do not assume that water is safe to drink
- If there is any doubt about the quality of the water, purify it
- Do not use unpurified water to clean your teeth, wash your mouth or wash your food with
- Do not drink sea water, urine, blood or the clear liquid found around

the eyes of animals and fish
- Conserve your body's water reservoir as much as possible
- Use rationing only in the most extreme circumstances
- When extracting water from vegetation and trees, do not drink any that is milky or dark in colour.

PART 5
Food

23. Fires for Cooking

As stated above, you can live without food for a considerable time, but you do need food in the long term for energy and in the short term for inner warmth. Food and drinks are obviously a lot more palatable if they are hot, but even cold food produces inner heat.

The lighting of fires is a subject that deserves a great deal of respect. It is not at all easy to light a fire and keep it going; it takes patience and effort; but the effort is well worth it in the end. I cannot emphasize enough the importance of a fire, as not only can you cook with it but also allows you to warm yourself in two other ways: first, by direct heat; and, second, by warming stones which can be placed inside your shelter and bedding. A fire will also have an enormous effect on morale and can lift a demoralized group in seconds.

A fire for cooking should be constructed in such a way that you can use it to cook food by different methods. If your cooking involves a lot of boiling, then the fire should be constructed to encourage flames, but if the meal involves roasting, then the fire should be constructed to produce heat from hot embers with little or no flame at all.

Matches and cigarette lighters
The first part of fire-lighting is to organize the method of ignition. In an ideal world, you would have a few boxes of matches with you, but in the real world of survival the chances are that you will only have a small box and that most of these will have been spent. Matches come in different sizes and quality; some light easily and can be struck on sandpaper or any other rough surface but others, known as safety matches, can only be struck on specially impregnated paper, although in the past I have managed to strike some on glass – albeit with difficulty. Good-quality matches have a strong wooden stem, while others have stems made from rolled paper, plastic or card; these can cause a lot of problems in a survival situation as they are far too flimsy, and either break as they are being

struck or burn out very quickly. All matches sold for household use suffer from the same problem: when they get damp they are impossible to light. If they are only slightly damp, then you can dry them a little by running them through your dry hair; do this several times and then strike them carefully, using as little force as possible. If they have gone past the slightly damp stage, do not bother to waste them by trying to light them: it is better to let them dry naturally; that way you still have a chance of lighting a fire with them at some stage.

Many survival-conscious enthusiasts create waterproof matches to add to their travel bag. The best way of doing this is to cover individual matches with a layer of wax – simply dripping wax from a candle over the matches will do the job. It is not sufficient just to cover the head of the match: the whole match should be covered to stop any damp from penetrating into the wooden stem and being sucked up to the head. Only use the red, 'strike-anywhere' matches for waterproofing, because safety matches need the special striker strip (which, incidentally, is no use if it gets wet).

Another simple way to achieve the waterproofing is to paint the matches with a coating of varnish; this can be the type of varnish you buy in the shops for DIY woodworking, or even nail varnish. It takes a long time to paint the individual matches, which should be fully covered, but the advantage of varnish is that once it is applied it stays in place until it is scraped away, whereas wax has a tendency to melt and run off the match (this is a particular problem when you are travelling in hot climates).

If you have gone to the trouble of waterproofing your matches, then you need to make sure that you keep them in a container that further helps with the waterproofing – a 35mm film carton is favoured by most survival experts as it holds a large quantity of matches and is also easily sealed. Standard-size matches are shorter than this type of container, and leave a space that can be used to store a little tinder material such as cotton wool.

Cigarette and cigar lighters can be purchased relatively cheaply and can be used again and again. Both gas- and petrol-fuelled types are ideal, although gas-fuelled lighters tend to freeze and become virtually inoperable at altitude. Obviously, you also need to bear in mind that the lighter flint and/or fuel will run out sooner or later.

FIRE LIGHTING

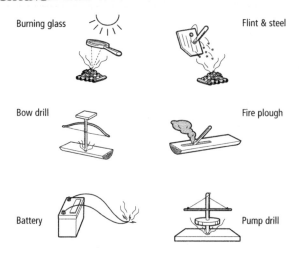

In the absence of matches and lighters, igniting fires is a time-consuming business. Everything must be ready and waiting before you begin to ignite the tinder.

Candles

Whether you use matches or lighters, you need to conserve them as much as possible, and one way of doing this is to light a candle. Once you light it, you can leave it to burn as long as you need to, whereas your matches and lighters would soon be spent with excessive use. If you do not have any candles, you can make a bundle of small twigs bound tightly together. Once the bundle has been lit, its tightness keeps it alight for some considerable time. Quite often the initial flames will give way to smouldering, which obviously slows down the burning process – when you want to use it to ignite your fire, all you do is blow onto it and the flames will reappear.

You can also manufacture your own candles using string as the wick and moulding animal fat around it. These home-made candles are nowhere near as good as the wax ones you can buy, but in a long-term survival situation using them to light your fires will save the life of your matches and lighters.

Batteries

Without matches or lighters, the task of creating a successful source of ignition comes down to sheer determination and patience. If you are lucky enough to have a vehicle battery around, then you can use this to ignite your fire – the bigger the battery, the better. Attach heavy wire to the terminals, and simply touch the ends of the wires together. However, be very careful how you do this: if the wire is too light, it will melt; in any event, the wire will become hot and can burn you – and, of course, there is always the risk of suffering an electric shock. Although it is better if the battery is a large powerful one, the principle will work even with ordinary small household batteries that are used in thousands of toys, torches and other items; simply stretch a strand of wire wool between the terminals and use the heat generated as the wire wool melts.

Burning lens

If you have no batteries, however, you will have to harness other power sources, such as the sun, which is the most powerful; if properly used, it can constitute an endless source of ignition. Clearly, the sunnier the day, the better the chances of success – if the sky is overcast, then there is no chance of lighting a fire with the sun's help.

Actually turning sunlight into fire requires the concentration of the sun's rays. This is best achieved by using a glass lens to concentrate the rays to heat your tinder sufficiently to ignite it – magnifying-glass lenses are ideal for this, and work very quickly, but other lenses such as those used in spectacles can also be used. You can also concentrate the sun's rays through broken glass, or a glass container filled with water.

Another proven method is to use a cone-shaped mirrored surface to concentrate the power. The most effective device for this is a torch lens: simply remove the bulb and place very dry, easily ignited tinder such as loose cotton wool at the base of the lens, and angle it so that the sun is shining straight into it; ensure that it is pointed exactly at the sun, and keep it there until ignition takes place.

Flint and steel

Many outdoor shops sell purpose-made flint and steel firelighters. They consist of an oversized cigarette-lighter flint attached to the side of a strip of wood, and a small section of hacksaw blade. The blade is run down the flint, causing hot sparks to shower down onto the tinder; this is a very simple process, but is nevertheless very effective. You can get the same result – although not so efficiently – by hitting a piece of natural flint with a knife.

Wood on wood

If you have been unfortunate enough to have arrived in a survival situation with virtually nothing, or have been living under survival conditions for so long that your resources have run out, you will have to rely on the environment to provide the whole of your fire-lighting equipment – involving a great deal of time, effort and muscle power.

Using friction to produce heat is difficult if you are not used to it, but it gets easier with time and experience. Essentially, you have to produce enough friction to heat a piece of wood to the point where it starts to burn, and the best way to achieve this is to prepare well before you begin. Firstly, you must make sure that the wood you use is as dead and as dry as possible; secondly, use a hardwood for the prime mover (male) and softwood for the recipient (female); the heat is generated by friction between the male and female, and the more friction you can create, the more productive the effort. Eventually, the friction will produce enough heat to start a fire. It is much easier if you carve a hollow in the softwood from both sides so that only a thin wafer of wood is left; by doing this, when the male piece enters and the movement begins, the paper-thin wood soon begins to burn at the edges. Adding tinder to this ember and blowing carefully will produce a flame.

Bamboo can be used in a similar way. Split a dead piece down the centre, and, using one half, cut a hole – making sure that the edges are shaved thin. Take a long strand of thin bamboo that fits neatly into the hole, and use it in a sawing action across the hole; once again, the more friction you can create the quicker the ignition.

The bow-drill

Make a simple bow using a fresh piece of green timber by tying strong string from tip to bottom (if you only have access to thin string, you can strengthen it by twisting strands of it together). The bow should be under a little tension, but not too much. Twist the string around the male hardwood timber, and place a piece of wood to use as a hand-pad over the top to steady it with; it will help if you carve a hollow in this piece of wood. To cut down on the friction at this point, you can use animal fat as a lubricant. Shaping the male timber into a point will also reduce the friction and help to keep it located in the hand-pad. In a piece of dry softwood, carve a round hollow in a conical shape at the edge and half way through the timber. Turn the softwood over and carve a second hollow to meet the first, making sure that there is a feather of thin wood at the base of the hollows. Enter the broad end of the hardwood male into the hollow and draw the bow back and forwards to cause the hardwood male to rotate. The process is quite easy, but the usual initial problem is gauging the amount of pressure in order to achieve the maximum amount of friction without the male sticking. Once this has been overcome, the rotating male will cause enough heat to ignite the feather of softwood; as soon as this happens, quickly remove the hardwood and blow into the female whilst holding a little fine, dry tinder against the ember until it bursts into flame.

The pump-drill

Although this piece of fire-lighting equipment takes time to manufacture, the effort is well worth it. Once again the male should be hard and the female soft. The male should ideally be approximately one metre in length and carved into a taper from 3cm (1¼in) in diameter at the top to 5cm (2ins) three-quarters of the way down its length, and finishing with a slight point at the tip. Carve a notch diagonally across the top of the male 2cm (¾in) deep and 0.5cm (¼in) wide. The next stage is to carve a flywheel, which can be done by taking a segment of tree from the trunk or thick branch approximately 30cm (1ft) in diameter and 8–10cm (3–4ins) thick. Carve a 4cm (1½in) hole in the centre of the segment. If you cannot cut a piece off the trunk, you can use a heavy log 15cm (6ins) thick and 30cm (1ft) long. Once this has been completed, the flywheel should be placed over the male and come to a halt as it meets the wider part of the male; tighten it by tapping it down. Use a green, fresh piece of timber 0.5m (18ins) long and 10cm (4ins) in diameter, and carve a hole half-way down its length at the midway point, tying a strong piece of string at the ends: this is the pump section. Place it over the top of the male, with the string seated in the carved groove; adjust the string so that the pump stops short of hitting the flywheel.

Place the male into the female (as described in *the bow drill* method). With one hand, hold the pump while turning the male so that the string twists around it, until the pump lifts to near the top of the male. Now put both hands on the pump and push sharply down, causing the string to unwind and straighten; the power exerted will quickly turn the male, throwing the flywheel around. At the point where the string fully unwinds, take the down pressure off allowing the flywheel to continue on its journey – thereby lifting the pump back to the top of the male as the string again twists around the male. Continue with the action until the friction created heats the female to burning point.

Building a fire

Having decided on the most suitable device with which to light a fire, you have to prepare the fire in advance of any ignition. One of the main reasons for failing to produce a decent fire in an economical way from the ignition stage is poor preparation. An outdoor fire requires a lot of fuel, which is required in three distinct stages.

The first is the tinder, which is best described as material that is easily combustible – the better the tinder, the easier the lighting procedure. Fine, open material such as fluffed-up cotton-wool is ideal tinder, especially if it is impregnated with an accelerant such as petrol. With this kind of tinder, it is easy to get it to burst into flame without too much trouble. The more tinder you collect, the better; as a minimum you will need enough to fill a soccer ball.

However, if you are not fortunate enough to have good-quality tinder available, you will have to find some in the local environment: very fine shavings from dry softwoods will suffice. Where birch trees are growing you can get very good tinder by peeling and using the fine paper-thin bark. Dry, dead leaves and grasses will all help. If you can find an empty birds' nest, the lining will make an excellent starter, progressing to the main nest as the flame builds.

Before lighting the tinder, however, you need a site for the main fire to move it on to the next stage. The second stage of fire lighting is to have available as large a pile of kindling as possible – enough to fill a medium-sized tent. This may seem excessive, but in fact it is the very minimum required for starting a fire and getting it sufficiently well established to take the larger fuel needed for continued warmth, cooking and purifying water. Kindling is made up of materials such as thin dead twigs and strips of old bark – none of which should be thicker than a pencil. However, if you are in a region where timber is scarce, you will have to make do with what you can find. In snow-covered regions, for example, you will have to dig under the snow to find your materials. Arrange a small pyramid of kindling mixed with tinder, leaving a small opening to put the burning tinder into. Do not put too much kindling on in the first place, as you may find that the fire will become starved of oxygen. This is especially true when too much grass and leaves are used; they tend to flare up very quickly, producing a spectacular flame, but then die away, leaving a mound of ashes that sap oxygen and stop the fire from properly taking hold of the thicker, more productive fuel. Adding kindling a little at a time is the best way of encouraging a decent fire – by doing this, the fire will have a good heart, making the best foundation for a good hot fire.

Once the kindling is alight and is burning productively (indicated by a minimum of smoke and a maximum of flame), the third stage of the operation can take place. This entails adding larger, heavier timber to the fire, and can be anything from 10cm (4ins) in diameter to full-grown tree trunks (if you can carry them!), the idea being that this type of fuel will burn for a long time and keep the fire going. Unfortunately, keeping a fire going indefinitely requires an enormous amount of fuel.

Once you have reached this stage, you can keep the fire going for as long as you have fuel; I have kept fires going in the most appalling conditions with rain pouring down on them, by covering the fire with a blanket of logs and earth, and then uncovering it when the rain has passed.

Fire building tips

Location
Choose a flat place that is out of the wind and as sheltered as possible. Make sure that it is not in a dangerous position or cannot easily spread out of control. Clear the ground: if there is a great deal of dead vegetation or a thick blanket of heather or other plant life, make sure you clear this to the actual ground level to stop the fire from spreading underneath, and out of sight. If the ground is wet or covered with snow and ice, build a raft with the heavier fuel and make the fire on this material; you can leave channels in the raft layer to encourage air to circulate under the fire to aid lighting. In flat locations where there is little cover from the wind, you should dig a trench for the fire to keep it from being blown out by the wind during the first lighting stage, and to conserve fuel later on.

If your shelter is within a cave, build your fire at the rear of the cave, so that the heat will take the majority of the smoke up to the roof, from where it will be sucked outside along the roof, keeping the lower living area a little less smoky. Unfortunately, fires and caves do not go well together, and no matter how much you try, you cannot get out of the smoke. Putting a fire in the mouth of the cave is even worse: if the wind blows your way, the whole of the cave fills with smoke and sparks. An exception to this is if you construct a wall behind the fire to stop the wind blowing the smoke in; a wall of this type can be made from rocks or large timbers, and act as a heat reflector. However, be careful that the rocks do not topple onto the fire and cause it to be knocked into the cave, or, if you are using timber, that it does not catch fire and send the fire out of control, blocking your escape from the cave. If you have any vehicle wreckage available, you may be able to use parts of it as a reflector, and if there is plenty of wreckage, large metal sheets can be used as underfloor heating. You can achieve this by laying a long length or several shorter lengths on the ground and covering them with a few centimetres of earth. Building your fire on the end of the sheet will heat the whole of it, transferring the heat under you; this is especially effective if the sheet is long enough to underpin your shelter (ensure that the fire is far enough away from your shelter to avoid your bedding going up in flames).

Fuel

The first stage is to gather enough tinder to begin the fire-lighting process. Keep it dry until you are ready to use it – putting it under your clothing helps. The next stage is to collect your kindling, which should be no thicker than a pencil, and enough fuel for a large bonfire. Once the fire is going well, it will even burn wet timber. When you are collecting, look up into the trees and bushes – dead timber that is off the ground even a few inches will be a lot drier than any you find on the floor.

Throughout your survival encounter you will become pre-occupied with finding fuel for the fire. If you manage to collect enough to stockpile, do not lay it on the ground; stand it upright either by resting it against a tree or rock, or by building it into a bonfire shape – by doing this, the rain will run off the steep surface and will not have time to remain on it until it soaks through.

Although I have concentrated on wood as the main fuel for a fire, there are alternatives. Other natural fuels that you can find include coal (usually found just under the surface), peat (which you will have to cut into small blocks and leave to dry for a couple of days before using), and sticky tar substances that are produced by naturally occurring petrochemicals (usually found in limestone areas). You can also use animal fats and animal dung; the fat will burn easily, but the dung needs to be dried first.

The best way of doing this is to gather it up by wrapping it in dead vegetation, and then stacking it off the floor to allow the air to dry it out.

Preparation

Get everything ready before you start to light a fire. You must have all the fuel close to hand, so that you can tend the fire and build it without having to leave it to find more fuel. Construct your fireplace to hold the particular design of fire you need. Build a platform for the fire to rest on and a surround to keep it contained, but do not use rocks and stones from river beds or from very wet locations, as these may have absorbed water and will explode when the water in them begins to boil and turns to steam. If you consider it to be too wet or too windy to light your fire, you are probably right. Waiting until the weather is more favourable will save you from wasting your precious fire-lighting capability.

Ignition

Where possible, conserve your matches and cigarette lighter by lighting a candle or bundle of twigs. Once the fire has been lit, make every effort to keep it going: letting it go out is unacceptable. Conserve your fuel by using it little and often. Use earth to dampen the fire, removing it to bring it back to life when you need the extra warmth, or for cooking and water purifying. Be ready to cover the heart of the fire when rain or snow threatens it.

FIRES FOR COOKING

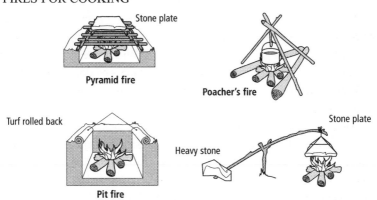

Different designs give the survivor a range of cooking methods, and keep fire under control.

Types of fire

There are many different designs of fire, each having a specific cooking, heating or water-purifying task. Some fires can be kept in for long periods, while others can be quickly extinguished and covered so as not to leave a trace of their existence. Fires can burn without the slightest amount smoke, giving a pure flame that shines brightly as a night-time signal, and provides an ideal water-boiling power, while others can be made to give off thick clouds of smoke, detectable for miles around during daylight hours (important for daylight signalling and for smoking and preserving food).

The type of fire you construct will depend on the food you need to cook and the environment in which you find yourself. Generally, one of the following fire designs will be sufficient.

The pit fire

Ideal for windy conditions, the pit fire is constructed by rolling back a section of turf and digging out a half-metre pit; placing a raft of timber at the bottom helps to stop any dampness from threatening the initial fire-lighting. Because the heat cannot escape from the sides of the fire, this design retains the heat well, and is especially good for cooking when there is not a great deal of fuel around – the concentrated heat uses less fuel, and allows you to keep the embers very hot, which is ideal for spit roasting. Because the fire is below the ground, you can place improvised cooking and boiling pots and pans over the fire without having to construct any elaborate framework. Once you have finished with the fire, it can be easily concealed by back-filling it and rolling the turf back over the pit; in a couple of days, the grass knits and soon reverts back to its natural state.

The pyramid fire

Starting with a shallow trench, you can construct a simple pyramid construction using fresh green timber. By keeping the actual fire low, the green timbers will not burn very quickly, and by placing a decent-sized flat stone or flat section of metal on top, you have a very effective hot-plate – ideal for melting animal fat and using frying methods to cook the food. If you have to use a flat stone as your hot-plate, do not use any stones that have been in a river, stream or very damp place, as they will explode when subjected to extreme heat.

Poacher's fire 1

This is a good fire to construct if you are using boiling as the main cooking method, or are using the fire to purify water. Once the fire has been lit in the normal way, lay two large pieces of fresh green timber to form a 'V' shape, so that the fire sits in the middle of the 'V' and the 'V' opening is positioned into the prevailing wind. Use three long, fresh, green timbers to form a high tripod-shape over the fire, and make a pan-hanger by using green timber with a natural spur. Hang your pan containing your water, stew, soup or whatever so that it hovers over the fire. Lay plenty of dry fuel on the fire directly below the pan; the wind being funnelled by the 'V' will soon fan the fire to the point where the fuel will produce high flames – ideal for boiling. If you want to regulate the flames a little, you can reposition the 'V' with the point into the wind, effectively cutting off the draught and reducing the flame height.

Poacher's fire 2

If you do not have a boiling pot, this fire allows you to cook your food by frying or baking. Having started the fire, you need a long pole of green, fresh timber and a piece of timber with a natural spur to act as pole rest. Attach a decent-sized flat stone to the long pole, and use it as a cooking plate. You can either keep the plate in the same position throughout the cooking process by placing a large rock to secure it, or you can adjust the height over the fire to speed up or slow down the cooking. Once the food is cooked, all you need to do is lift the plate out of the fire and you can eat straight off it.

24. Cooking Methods

A number of cooking methods help to vary the survival diet – in long-term survival, having some variety aids morale. Wherever possible, wrap your food in aluminium foil or cook it in a container in order to reduce the risk of it shrivelling and to conserve the juices. Baking in mud is an excellent way of cooking: you should completely cover the food with a thick layer, and let it dry before placing it in the embers of the fire or digging it in under the fire. If there is plenty of dried grass around, you can start by wrapping the food in the grass before covering it with mud; the dried grasses give the food a unique flavour. Give the parcel enough time for the mud to be baked hard all the way through before removing it from the heat.

Roasting meat, fish and root vegetables on a spit is another good way of cooking. A roasting fire should have embers, not flames, otherwise the flames will catch the food and cook it from the outside, leaving the inside raw. Slowly rotating the food will ensure that the food is fully cooked, but if your spit is made from wood, you must use strong, green timber to reduce the chance of it burning through before your food is cooked.

Smoking food may seem a little over the top for survival cooking; however, it not only gives the food a pleasant alternative taste but, if carried out properly, it will preserve food by impregnating and covering it with a layer of carbon. Quick smoking leaves a thin layer of carbon on the outside of the food, but does not preserve the inside. To preserve the food thoroughly it should be slowly smoked, allowing the carbon to penetrate deep into the flesh. You should only use hardwoods for smoking fuel, as the smoke from softwood can cause cancer.

The correct methods of cooking wild foods will make these foods more palatable and reduce the chances of stomach-upsets and food poisoning.

If you are in any doubt, the most effective and safest way to cook food is to dice it into very small pieces and boil it.

Crustaceans
The simplest method of cooking crustaceans is to boil them. They require only a little cooking time, and once they have been cooked they should be consumed immediately, as they will soon begin to go off.

Fish
All cooking methods are suitable for fish. Fresh-water fish are better if they are boiled for a short time to remove the earthy taste, before cooking by any other method. Fish are particularly suitable for preserving by smoking – the longer they are left in the smoke, the drier and harder they become, extending their shelf-life.

Reptiles
Smaller ones are best toasted, while snakes and turtles should be cut into small segments and boiled.

Small game
These may be cooked whole or in joints. If you are unsure about the tenderness quality of the flesh, boil it before roasting.

Roots
These are often very tough and require slow baking, roasting or boiling.

Pot herbs
Always boil these items. In some cases it may be wise to boil them in one, two or even three changes of water to remove undesirable, strong-tasting acids.

Fruits
Eat succulent, soft varieties raw, but bake the thick-skinned, tougher types.

25. Primitive Equipment

In our everyday lives, we take so much for granted. Imagine not having a knife and fork to eat with, or trying to cook without utensils and pots and pans. In a survival situation, the chances are that you will not have any of these necessities. It is extremely difficult to manufacture the basics without a knife or small hatchet, but it is not impossible. You may be able to fashion simple tools and cooking equipment from any wreckage, or perhaps by adapting the items you are carrying with you. For example, the air-filter housing on most cars, lorries and 4 x 4 vehicles would make a good frying-pan or saucepan. Metal wheel hubcaps can be used as boiling pans, and plastic ones can be used as plates. Parts of the vehicle's wiring loom can be stripped, and once the outer plastic cover is burned off the wire can be used to construct simple wire hangers that can be used to secure pans and other receptacles over the fire while food is being cooked. If there are no pans, simply use the wire to skewer your food and dangle it in the heat of the fire.

If you can cut a section out of large bamboo, you can use the sealed section between its segments to boil water in or to cook food. Knocking the segments through in small bamboo makes very effective straws, while the very thin varieties of bamboo and other smooth pencil-like wood can be used as chopsticks. Not only will this save you from burning your fingers, but it will also ensure that you are not eating the filth and bacteria that will be building up on your hands and fingers (no matter how often you wash your hands, they continue to become very dirty in survival situations, and in any event, the water you use to wash with will not be safe unless you have purified it first!).

EQUIPMENT

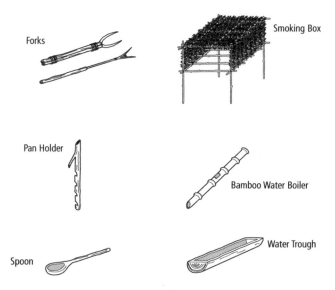

Forks

Smoking Box

Pan Holder

Bamboo Water Boiler

Water Trough

Spoon

In a survival situation you soon realize how much you take for granted in everyday life: without the basic tools, cooking and eating become a major problem.

26. Hunting/Traps and Trapping

Hunting

Before you can eat wild animals, birds or fish, you have to catch them! This is best done by trapping them. Running around with a home-made spear is not a very productive way to hunt your food, although you may have to resort to this method if there is no alternative. Whatever method you use to catch your prey, always ensure that you kill it quickly and effectively with the minimum amount of distress to the animal.

You may have to stalk your quarry – that is, follow and approach it with stealth and complete quietness. If you have never done this before, I can tell you that it is not easy. The following tips will help you:

- When stalking, approach your prey with the prevailing wind in your face; all wild animals have a keen sense of smell, and even on a calm day air currents will carry human scent a very long way.
- Where possible, try to keep the sun behind you – especially when it is low in the sky; animals do not see well when they are looking into bright sunlight.
- In wooded country, move very slowly and avoid standing on and snapping twigs. Be on the lookout for low branches and foliage that you may be caught up in, or that will make a noise when you brush against it. Animals only make a noise in woodland when they take flight because of danger; other animals, hearing this, assume that danger is approaching and go to ground.
- In mountainous areas, noise from falling rocks is common and rarely spooks game, unless there is too much of it.
- Approach grazing animals from a higher position, as they don't usually experience a threat from this quarter, and therefore tend to keep a watch lower down the slopes.
- In snow-covered areas, hunt in soft, fresh snow, as crisp snow and ice echoes for quite a distance when crushed or broken underfoot, putting any local game on its guard.
- When tracking game, keep off their trails: all wild animals constantly watch their back trails.
- When constructing traps and fishing lines, ensure that you disturb the local area as little as possible.

Trapping

Trapping is the most productive way of keeping you from starving. There are very few areas of the world where there are no animals, birds or fish to eat: the problem is being able to locate them and then catching them. Although you may have some luck with a home-made bow and arrow or spear, the chances are that you will spend a lot of time making these weapons and a lot more time trying to be accurate enough with them to kill enough food for a meal. Unless you have some knowledge of the outdoor scene beforehand, you may well be using more energy locating and killing your game than you get from eating it! Trapping also takes time and skill, but once traps are set they are working for you even when you are fast asleep. That's not to say that you should not try your hand at hunting with weapons, though: nothing ventured, nothing gained.

Trapping to survive means that you will have to adapt yourself quickly to the task. Being successful is about practice and patience. Your first trapping attempts may not be very productive, but with time and experience there is no reason why you should not be able to keep yourself and others supplied with enough food to survive until you are rescued.

Trapping is a skilful business. The basis of successful trapping consists of good preparation, planning and patience. Even with no experience of trapping, you can make a simple trap and catch local game. Luck plays a big part in early trapping experiences, as most people do not know where to find game or how to set the traps properly. In time these skills will become second nature, and as a result your food supplies will be assured. During early trapping expeditions, it will help if you think about what you are trying to achieve and keep in mind the following simple rules.

Animals, birds and fish spend the whole of their lives avoiding predators, especially man! Because of this they have very sharp senses, and quickly recognize and react to smells, sound and movement that they are not used to. Man's scent is very distinctive: keeping your scent away from trapping areas and equipment is the first rule of good trapping. Where possible, use streams and other water features to travel to and from your traps; water does not hold scent well, and if it's running, it will mask the noise of your approach. Crushed vegetation gives off a strong odour; a little is expected, but when there is a lot of disturbance animals become increasingly wary, and will go around the hazard even if it is on their usual trail. If this is the case, do not go back to the trap or move it: leave it in position and check it regularly from a distance. Once the ground re-establishes itself and the hazard passes, the game will use the trail again. If your shelter is made from wreckage, and/or if you are using oil and fuel for fire-lighting, keep your trapping equipment, footwear and clothing well away from the shelter area. Even tiny amounts of oil and fuel leave a strong scent that will linger in and around the trap areas for a very long time. No game will stay in an area where there is a scent that they are not used to, so keeping traps odour-free is the best way to ensure that you continue to trap your food successfully. Where possible, leave your traps in the trapping location and hunting areas, which should be well away from the campsite. If you have to move the traps, store them well outside the camp area, and if they become contaminated by any human source, you can decontaminate them by hanging them in the smoke of the camp fire. Game are used to the smell of smoke, and soon come back into the hunting area when they realize that there is no fire present.

When you have set your traps, use a very light covering of local vegetation to camouflage them. However, do not rip up the grass or break leaves off trees and bushes, as this defeats the object; use camouflage that you can find without disturbing the immediate trapping location. Avoid using too much camouflage as this may foul the trap or spring it prematurely. Also, avoid building traps directly on the ground: you cannot hope to catch game by expecting it to climb onto a trap. Well-set trail traps should be dug in slightly below the normal ground level. In winter conditions, frost can freeze the trap-triggers, keeping them from being tripped. In these conditions it may be more productive if you change trigger-trapping designs to snares. A professional trap will kill its prey in a split-second, without the creature knowing anything about it.

Unfortunately, inexperienced trapping techniques can cause animals to suffer. I have often seen animals caught by their legs or half-way down their bodies by badly positioned snares. Not killed outright as they should have been, the animals have pulled, turned and twisted in their attempts to break free, leaving them cut and stripped to the bone. On rare occasions, even experienced trappers have traps that have partly failed, catching – but not killing – the animal. In these situations you should take great care approaching the trapped animal: even an animal near to death can give you a serious injury. The only way to deal safely with the animal is to kill it using a heavy, hard pole or iron bar known as a priest; this should be used by hitting the creature on the back of the neck with enough force to break it. If you think you have only stunned it, make sure by pushing the point of a sharp knife through the creature's neck behind the windpipe and cutting towards the back of the neck. This will cut through the main arteries and quickly dispatch the animal.

Bird traps

One of the simplest ways of trapping large seed-eating birds is to bait a fish-hook with seed or a piece of fruit and secure it to a strong fishing line, making sure the line is tied off securely. Throw a few seeds around the area, and a bird will peck at the bait and become caught on the fish-hook.

If you do have fishing line, look for an area where birds roost or where there are plenty of nests. Tie lengths of the line to the branches to secure them and then tie running nooses on all the lines. Birds will land on the branches and step into the nooses, getting their feet caught and stopping them from escaping.

One of my favourite bird-traps is the spring snare. This is particularly good for catching large ground-feeding game birds such as pheasants. The spring should be a young sapling with plenty of power. Tie two pieces of twine, cord or heavy fishing line to a sapling; bend the sapling down so that the strings touch the ground, and mark the spot where it touches. Let the sapling return to its original position. Carefully dig a hole approximately 10cm (4ins) in diameter and 15cm (6ins) deep, and knock a securing peg deep in the centre of the hole; secure a second peg to the string leading from the sapling. Tie a snare to the second line attached to the sapling. Push the securing peg through the snare, and pull the sapling down so that the securing peg meets the peg in the hole, and connect the two pegs together by cutting interlocking grooves to form the trigger. Pull the snare out so that it encircles the hole; spread a little bait around the area, finishing with a plentiful supply of bait in the hole. The game bird will take the bait from around the hole and eventually put its head in the hole to take the bait; this will dislodge the peg trigger, at which point the spring of the sapling will straighten, lifting the snare and taking the bird, breaking its neck as it snatches it off the ground.

Water-fowl trap

The stilt duck trap is simple in its construction and operation, and was first described to me some years ago by Eddie McGee, a former British paratrooper and one of the UK's leading survival and tracking experts. In shallow water take three straight pieces of timber and form them in a tripod-shape below the water level. Attach either a simple snare or float and baited fish-hook to a heavy, flat stone, and balance the rock on top of the tripod. The trap is sprung when the water-fowl swims up to take the bait. Once it has been caught, it will panic; kick the tripod and dislodge the stone, which will obviously sink, dragging the head of the fowl underwater and holding it there until it drowns.

Fish traps

The best known of all fish traps is the fishing rod, which is very easy to make and use. The rod should be made from a fresh, young sapling, 2–3m

(6–9ft) long. Fish will take any bait if it looks appetising – strips of silver paper, feathers and pieces of metal shaped like the bowl of a teaspoon and slowly pulled across the water all have the potential to catch fish. Live bait can be easily found by digging worms, or stripping the bark away from dead trees and collecting the insects that hide and live there.

In tidal waters, constructing a wall can make a very effective trap. The idea behind this is that as the water recedes a reservoir is created, holding the fish. The wall should be horseshoe-shaped approximately one metre high at the highest point and graded to ground level at each end, and the opening should face the land. Tides can be a strong force, so the rocks used in the wall's construction should be heavy enough not to be easily dislodged. Obviously the trap will be covered by water at high tide and exposed during low tide, when it should be checked.

Small game traps

The snare is the easiest trap to construct and use, and can be very productive. A snare is nothing more than a loop with a running knot to form a noose – the idea being that the animal puts its head through the noose, tightening it as it runs and snapping its neck to kill it. Snares can be made from many different materials: strong string, animal sinew, strands of animal skin, heavy fishing line, or any material that is flexible enough to form the noose, supple enough to tie the running knot and strong enough to hold the animal. The snare should be firmly secured to an immovable object – saplings and other deep-rooted branched vegetation are ideal – and set along an animal trail. For rabbits the noose should be approximately 14cm (5½ins) in diameter and set so that the bottom of the noose is 14cm (5½ins) from the ground –or the size of one adult fist with the thumb straightened. For hares, the bottom of the noose should be 19cm (16ins), or the size of an adult hand-span with the little finger stretched and touching the ground and the thumb stretched high. Hares run head-up – hence the difference in height; any lower and the animals will either run over the snares or get their legs caught; any higher and the animals will run under the snare.

Hedgehogs make good food and can easily be caught in a bucket trap, made by digging a hole 30cm (1ft) in diameter and 30cm (1ft) deep. The sides of the hole should be undercut (sloping inwards) so that the animal cannot climb out. Use a little animal fat to bait the trap: the hedgehog will climb in to eat the bait but will not be able to escape.

TRAPS

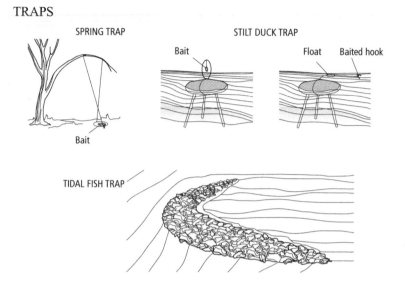

Being able to make simple traps will ensure that you can catch enough food to aid your survival.

27. What to Eat

All free running game is safe to eat, as are birds' eggs. Some taste better than others, but taste becomes less of a problem as you become hungrier! However, never be tempted to eat anything that you find dead, and avoid an animal that makes little or no effort to avoid capture, as it is probably dying through illness or poison anyway – either way you do not want to risk the same fate.

Once you have killed your prey, leave it to hang for a while to give the body heat time to disperse: eating meat and fish when it is too fresh can cause stomach-upsets.

Seafood is a good source of protein but tends to deteriorate quickly once exposed to the air. Many fish, especially in the tropics, have poison spines and skin; therefore avoid fish with spines or those that are particularly ugly, such as scorpion, porcupine, file, and zebra.

Other edible seafoods include snails, clams, muscles, limpets, sea urchins, sea cucumber, scallops and star-fish. The majority of seaweed is also safe to eat either raw or cooked. Before resorting to eating seaweed, however, make sure that you have an adequate supply of fresh water, as it takes a lot of water in the body to properly digest it. You should only eat fresh seaweed, which will be firm to the touch, smooth and have no offensive odours. Some varieties are very high in irritant acids, and you can tell if this is the case by crushing it: if it is high it will go 'off', and omit an offensive odour within ten minutes. If this is the case, boil it in at least two changes of water to remove the acid.

Preparing the kills for the pot

Fish

Having used your priest to dispatch the fish, scrape off any scales by holding the fish's tail and scraping with the back of a knife or sharp stone down towards the head; this is best done in water so that the scales can be washed off as you work. Once the scales have been removed, hold the fish by its head so that its stomach is facing upwards; with the point of the knife, insert it just below the head and cut the fish towards the tail, ending just before it. The cut should be deep enough to cut through the flesh, but not so deep that it severs the innards; scrape the cavity clean, leaving none of the stomach within. The head can be removed by cutting behind the gills, and the tail and fins can all be cut away. Remove the fins and gills of flat fish, ut the stomach, which is situated just below the head on the dark side of the fish, and clean the innards out. The head can be removed by cutting in a semicircle below it. If you prefer your fish skinned, keep it very wet and make a cut through the skin just above the tail, without cutting into the flesh. Hold the tail tightly and peel the skin back a little; press down on the backbone, and continue to peel the skin carefully to ensure that the flesh is not removed with the skin.

Small birds

Holding the bird firmly in one hand, use the thumb and first finger of your free hand to take a few feathers at a time and pluck them out – if you take too many feathers at once, you risk ripping the flesh. Don't bother to pluck the neck and head. Once this is completed, cut off the head and neck just above the breast, and cut the legs off by slicing through the joint at the knee. Lie the bird on its back and cut a circle around the anus: the cut should be just deep enough to cut through the flesh, and care should be taken not to cut into the innards. Once the cut has been made, pull the flesh down, push your second finger into the cavity and over the top of the innards, keeping the back of your finger close to the breast bone. When the finger is fully inserted, bend it over the back of the innards and draw it out, using it to scoop out the whole of the innards, which will come away very easily. If possible wash the bird inside and out, making sure that there are no innards remaining inside.

Large birds

A similar process applies to large birds – the difference being the size and weight involved. Plucking a large bird is best done by placing it on your lap, with its neck and head between your knees and holding its feet together with one hand; from this position you can easily pluck the bird clean. Once the anus is cut, you will have to push the whole of your hand inside the body cavity and scrape the innards out.

In both of the above cases, you can pluck the birds over a hole and place the feathers in it as you pluck, which will stop the feathers from being blown around. Once the bird is fully plucked, gather the feathers and use them for insulation. If you don't need the innards for trap and fish bait, scrape them directly into the hole and bury them. If you can distinguish the heart and liver, keep these and cook them with the bird.

Game

Once the animal has been dispatched, it is best if you hang it by its rear legs with its belly facing you. Use the tip of your knife to cut through the skin only: do not cut into the flesh. The best way is to pinch a little fur/skin near to one of the rear feet and pull it away from the leg. Make a small cut horizontally, stopping when you have gone through the skin. Insert the point of your knife from above with the back of the knife facing in towards the flesh. Carefully slice the skin down the length of the leg, finishing at the top centre of the body. Carry out the same procedure on the other leg, making sure the cut joins the first to form a 'V' shape. From the bottom of the 'V', continue cutting the skin down the centre of the animal, stopping at the head. When you have done this, use the knife to cut the skin from around the legs. Using the same technique as for the rear legs, skin the front legs, then cut the skin away from around the stomach. From the rear of the animal, pull the skin down exposing the body flesh, stopping when it reaches the head; cut it away from the body and save it for stretching and drying.

Cut the animal open by inserting the point of your knife above the rib cage sufficiently deep to cut the flesh, but not so deep that it cuts the innards. Run the knife up to open the whole stomach; place your hands inside the body cavity and pull out the innards. When you have done this, cut or chop through the centre of the breastbone and pull out the lungs and heart, which will be attached to the windpipe and head. Pull them down and remove the head.

SKINNING GAME

Knife cuts --------

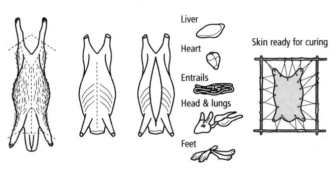

Liver

Heart

Entrails

Head & lungs

Feet

Skin ready for curing

Once the kill is skinned and gutted, the meat should be hung until the natural body heat has dispersed before you can eat it.

Rats

You can find and easily trap rats in most places – using your other kills' entrails as bait helps. Rats make good eating, but have to be prepared with great care and precision when removing the innards – this is true of all your kills, but with rats it is even more important. Because they are relatively small, they are difficult to handle. During skinning and gutting, you should ensure that no urine is discharged due to poor cutting or killing techniques, as rats carry the disease *leptospirosis* – commonly known as 'rat catcher's yellows' – in their urine. *Spirochaete* bacteria cause the disease, which shows jaundice symptoms – hence the 'yellow' reference. It's a very dangerous disease, and you should guard against it at all times.

Having satisfied yourself that the rat is clean, the best way to cook it is to roast it slowly over hot embers, or have it boned, diced and boiled.

Snails and earthworms

Both snails and earthworms make good eating and are full of protein.

Worms can be washed, boiled and eaten straight away, although you may find them more palatable if you chop them up into small sections and mix them with other food; they're particularly good with eggs.

Snails need a little preparation before they can be consumed. The meat is fine to eat, but snails can eat plant life that is poisonous to humans, so their intestines and stomach need to be cleared of any poisons before you eat them (gutting them is impracticable). The most effective way of doing this is to purge the snails by keeping them in a container and feeding them with fresh vegetation that is safe for humans to eat: great plantain (*Plantago major*) is ideal for this. If you have any of the mints available such as corn mint (*Mentha arvensis*) or spearmint (*Mentha spicata*), a little added to their diet will give the snails a good clean taste. You should keep them in the container for two or three days before cooking them whole by placing them into a pan of boiling water.

There are several well-documented instances where survivors have had to resort to eating human flesh to save them from dying of starvation. It is widely accepted around the world that in exceptional circumstances such as survival, cannibalism will not carry a criminal penalty. This does not mean that a person will be forgiven if he/she kills another human for food: that would be an act of murder. However, if the person had died from injuries sustained from an accident or hypothermia, then eating the dead person's flesh is acceptable. Whether or not you could bring yourself to do this in a life-or-death situation is clearly a matter for you, and can only really be decided at the time. But consider whether you would want your colleagues to live by eating your flesh if you were the dead person. Would it matter? Obviously, if you ever have to resort to such a drastic course of action, then counselling will be available afterwards.

If you are ever faced with this situation and have decided to eat the flesh, then the body and meat has to be dealt with in the same way as any other game.

Poisonous animals
As discussed earlier, all free running game is safe to eat. However, eating too much rabbit with no other food can lead to a vitamin deficiency that can cause death. The livers of polar bears and bearded seals are also poisonous at certain times of the year. The rarest killer disease in the world is laughing sickness, which is contracted by eating human brain.

28. Edible/Medicinal Plants

Nature has provided us with an abundance of edible plant life. Unfortunately, there are no indicators to differentiate the edible ones from the poisonous ones. As a result, in a survival situation you need to be extra careful before eating something that you do not recognize.

In general terms, do not eat any plant that has a milky sap. Brightly coloured fruits, especially those that are bright red, should be avoided. You should work on the basis that the plant's purpose is to survive and reproduce; given this, why would it make itself so available to be eaten? – probably because it's full of poison. There are exceptions I know, but if you do not recognize the plant, leave it alone.

As a young boy growing up, I used to go for walks with my father. Like most of the other members of our family, he would pick plants from the fields to use in the preparation of herbal remedies. The lessons I learnt then have stayed with me, and even now I often revert to simple home-made remedies to solve everyday medical problems. In fact, my daughters will still ask me for simple remedies – despite the fact that they have left home, and that one is a qualified nurse.

Unfortunately, it is beyond the scope of this book to list and explain the thousands of edible and medicinal herbs throughout the world. Nevertheless the following is a short list to demonstrate the diversity of edible and medicinal plants.

Great plantain (*Plantago Major*)
This perennial herb was one of my father's favourites – I used to have to pick it by the bucketful. He would boil it and drink an eggcupful of the juice three times a day as a tonic to cure boils. We also used the leaves warmed and wrapped around sprains and aching limbs. My grandmother would soak the leaves overnight and use the liquid as a cough remedy, while her oldest son, my uncle, dried the leaves and rolled them into cigarettes when he had no money to buy his favourite brand. He claimed that smoking the leaves helped his breathing…

Rosebay Willow Herb (*Chamaenerion angustifolium*)
Also known as fireweed, the young leaves can be used in salads, and the roots can be use as a tasty vegetable. The younger the plant the better.

Stinging nettle (*Urtica dioica*)

I've already mentioned the fact that this plant is excellent for making rope and fine string. The leaves make very good eating too, looking and tasting like spinach; picking them can be an obvious problem, but shouldn't be too bad if you have a pair of gloves. Leather is best, as the sting of nettles is very potent and can permeate the heaviest woollen gloves and clothing. All the leaves can be eaten, but tender young ones are slightly sweeter. Once you have picked them, the leaves should be placed in boiling water for 15 minutes and the water discarded; this gets rid of the acid. Pour on some fresh water and bring to the boil. You can eat the leaves as they are, add them to stews or fry them with a little animal fat.

Medicinally, nettle is a valuable plant. Thick soup made with the youngest leaves is good for purifying the blood. My grandmother suffered from rheumatism for most of her adult life, and used to tell me that if she nettled herself the symptoms reduced for a time. I have never tried this remedy, but I did have the whole of my body covered with nettle stings on one occasion. Once the initial pain and itching had worn off, I did not experience any adverse effects, and despite the fact that I had been pushing my body very hard at the time, I did not have any of the normal aches and pain normally associated with very strenuous exercise.

Hawthorn (*Rosaceae crataegus monogyna*)

Perhaps the best way to demonstrate the diversity of plant life and the way in which it can be used in a survival situation is to look at the properties of this bush.

I have often picked and eaten hawthorn leaves to freshen my mouth. As well as the leaves, the bright red haws can be eaten raw, or cooked and used in salads and stews. Although they have no distinct taste, they do make excellent jam and preserves.

Medicinally, its main value is its effect as a cardiac sedative: it dilates the blood vessels, thereby reducing blood pressure; the parts used for this are the dried flowers and the fresh or dried haws. About two handfuls of these should be soaked in a little water overnight and two teaspoonsful of the resulting liquor added to a cup of water and left standing for 15 minutes. The resulting medicine should be taken two to four times a day for several weeks, as it will take this amount of time to begin to work properly. Compote made by adding the fruit to syrup made from the flesh of haws mixed with honey can be given for diarrhoea.

The wood has a hard brown heart, and is strong enough to be used to make tools and trap-triggers.

As a weather indicator, the saying, "Ne'er cast a clout, before May is out," is a well-known warning against the possibility of a late cold spell, and is a reference to the hawthorn's display of white flowers. When there is an abundance of haws it indicates a hard, cold winter; I have used this sign for many years, and it hasn't let me down yet.

In a survival situation, you will need to use whatever knowledge you have in order to get the best out of the environment you are faced with. Thinking laterally about the possible uses of plants and other available items is an important skill. The more you can gain from your surroundings, the better your chances. Remember: nothing ventured, nothing gained.

PART 6
Surviving People

29. On Foot

Hitchhiking

If your travel plans involve getting lifts from people who offer them, you should begin by recognizing that you are setting yourself up to become a target. That's not to say that you shouldn't go ahead and do it, but you should understand the pitfalls and be aware of some of the ways to protect yourself and survive. Whether you are female or male, do not travel alone – having a travelling partner will help to reduce the risk of you becoming a victim. Be under no illusion, attackers come in all shapes, sizes, creeds, colours and genders: even if you are with a partner, think twice before accepting a lift in a vehicle with more than one young male in it.

Plan your journey well before you go. Make sure that you know a little about the customs and practices of the countries you are going to visit or pass through. Plan your route in such a way that you can circumnavigate unfriendly parts of the world and war zones.

Dress down for the journey; wearing clothing that exposes too much flesh is dangerous and provocative – as well as being illegal in many countries. Likewise, wearing a sports shirt or anything else that proudly displays your country's flag will attract the unwanted attention of every political, religious and xenophobic extremist for miles around.

Cities and towns

If you are carrying luggage, you are probably a tourist; consequently, you will be seen and targeted by any local criminals that make their living from theft. Pickpockets are the ones you will probably encounter first; by the very nature of their work they need to get close enough to you to pick your pockets. Spreading your money, valuables and official paperwork around your body will lessen the chances of everything you own going in one dip. If you have buttons on your pockets, keep them fastened; do not keep your wallet or purse in your back trouser pocket – even if it has a fastener: the outline of these items draws the thieves' attention; keep jackets and coats fastened tightly. If you are wearing jewellery, take it off and stow it away until you reach your destination.

Carrying luggage

If your luggage, purses or handbags have straps, use them. Keep all your baggage with you all the time, and if you have to put it down either stand astride it, sit on it or place your foot through the straps. Where luggage has external pockets, avoid using them to store valuables, passports, credit cards and purses. Keep all of your baggage in front of you, and close enough to be able to retrieve it very quickly. In some countries, criminals work in groups and will try to put themselves between you and your luggage, separating you from it. Once this happens, a second group will take the bags, passing them on from thief to thief. Where there are crowds, be extra vigilant, although this is not as easy as it may seem. If you have ever been to India, you will understand what it is like trying to keep begging children at bay: there are so many children around you, that you are virtually stopped from walking. The worst thing you can do is to open your purse and hand out cash – once you do this the flood-gates open, and a wave of street urchins pours out along with the thieves. The only way to avoid this is to ignore them in the first place – it's difficult, but your safety has to come first.

Muggings and armed assault

There isn't a lot to say about these types of violent assault, except to advise you to keep as calm as you can and hand over whatever the assailants want as quickly as possible. The chances are that the items or money they are after can be replaced – your life cannot, and that is what really matters.

30. Transport: self-drive and public

Where travelling involves driving a vehicle, make sure that you have checked or have had the vehicle checked and serviced regularly: there is no excuse for putting yourself at risk by driving around in a vehicle that is not up to the job. All vehicles will break down at some stage – usually when you least expect it – so being a member of a recognized breakdown service is an absolute necessity. While you are waiting for assistance, protect yourself by keeping the doors and windows locked. If you have broken down on a motorway, clear the vehicle and stand off the hard shoulder. For lone females, it's worth carrying a pair of overalls in the boot of the car, along with any headgear typically worn by men; dressed in this way with your hair hidden, hopefully you will be seen as male, which will lessen the risk of any unwanted attention.

Car-jacking

When driving around in your vehicle, you can be lulled into a false sense of security. However, always make sure that you drive around with your doors locked. I am aware that some people believe that keeping the doors locked may hamper their escape following an accident. Think of it this way, though: you can easily unlock the doors after the event. If you can't, then those who assist you can simply smash a window and get you out.

There are several ways in which cars are hijacked. A favourite method involves the hijackers waiting near to a filling station. Many people fill their vehicle with fuel while leaving the ignition keys in the vehicle, and having filled the vehicle with fuel they go to pay for it allowing, the thieves the opportunity to take the vehicle. You should lock your vehicle every time you leave it – no matter how short a time you expect to be away. Another ploy is for a team of hijackers to follow a vehicle they want and to stage a minor accident by crashing into the rear of the target vehicle at an isolated road junction. Obviously the driver will then get out to view the damage, allowing the hijackers to make off with the vehicle. To avoid this, make sure that you continually check your rear-view mirrors and monitor the traffic following you. If there is a vehicle that has two or more occupants and which has been behind you for some time, be cautious. It may be worth turning the car around and going in the opposite direction to see if they still follow you. However, if you do decide to do this, make sure you can turn around without having to stop and reverse; you should also ensure that you do not turn into a dead-end. If you are involved in a minor accident and are unsure about the situation, stay in your vehicle, keeping the doors and windows shut. Let the other party involved get out and come to you. If they want your insurance details, shout them; likewise, they can communicate their details in the same way. Do not open the window to speak to them, as they can easily grab you or your keys – even if you open it just a little, they can get their fingers over the glass and force it down; keep your engine running and be ready to drive away if the situation becomes threatening. Once you have left the scene, drive to the nearest police station and report the incident: this should alert the police to the hijackers, and demonstrate that you did not intend to leave the scene of an accident and were merely in fear of your safety.

When you are in your vehicle, make sure that all your valuables are out of sight. Opportunist thieves will open passenger doors, enter through open windows or smash a window to grab mobile telephones, wallets, purses, laptop computers or any other carried items they take a fancy to when you are stopped at crossroads and traffic lights. Keeping everything out of sight removes the target: no target, no crime, no threat – simple!

Where the thief or attacker has entered the car through a window or open door, and you fear for your safety, you can use your ice-scraper to jab their hand or face to force them out, or you can spray de-icer into their eyes. If you have to resort to this type of action, make sure you are ready to pull away as soon as the attacker has pulled back from the vehicle.

Where you are waiting in traffic, leave a gap between you and the vehicle in front large enough to allow you to manoeuvre out of trouble if need be.

Evasive driving

If you consider that you are being followed, or you know you are being pursued by another vehicle, then you will have to adopt evasive driving techniques. For the most part, your ability to get away will be determined by the vehicles involved. In any event, you should move your vehicle to take up a position in the middle of the road with a slight bias towards the passenger side of the road – a following vehicle will have to pull onto the wrong side of the road for the driver to see if it is safe to pass. If there are oncoming vehicles, the pursuing driver will continually be forced back behind you, while keeping slightly over to the passenger side stops him from passing you on the inside. Where there are bends and you can see a long way in front of you, cut across the bends keeping as straight a line as possible; this will help you to negotiate bends at speed and stop the pursuing vehicle from cutting a bend to force you off the road. Throughout any period of evasive driving, keep your car in lower gears as much as possible, as this will increase your engine control and acceleration – once you select top gear or overdrive, you lose an element of control. Keep both hands on the wheel all the time, and do not wrap your hands around your thumbs inside the wheel – if your front wheels hit a kerb or some other prominent object at speed, the sudden jerk of the steering-wheel can be very powerful, and with your thumbs on the inside the wheel's cross-member can dislocate your thumbs. Keep your braking to a minimum and avoid sharp braking; use your gears to slow down. Smoothly operating the accelerator will help you to control your speed without losing road grip. And if you have never carried out an evasive handbrake turn, the middle of a pursuit is not the time to try it.

Beware the flat tyre

In many cars the spare wheel is situated in the boot. When you are touring or when you have been shopping, you also lock your luggage in the boot. Organized gangs target vehicles parked in restaurant car parks that they recognize as being from hire companies or displaying out-of-area registration plates. Having selected a suitable vehicle, they let one of the tyres down, either by letting it down completely in the car park, or by inserting a match-stick in the valve, holding it open just enough to let the air out slowly. In either case, when the tyre is flat the occupants are forced to stop in order to change the wheel, and because the spare wheel is in the boot, the luggage has to be taken out. At this stage, the gang is in position to snatch the luggage and make off with it. In some cases the gang may follow the target vehicle until it has to stop; they may even pull over and offer to help to change the wheel, while helping themselves to your luggage at the same time.

If you own a vehicle with a spare wheel in the boot, consider taking it out of its holder and placing it on top of your luggage so that in the event of a flat tyre you don't have to unload everything to get to it. With hire vehicles, ask the hirer if you can have a vehicle that has the spare stored in a carrier outside the boot. The other alternative is to call for roadside assistance to change the wheel for you.

Public transport

Taxis

I can think of two incidents when I was in fear of my life while being transported in so-called taxis. The first was in the Transylvanian Alps in Romania, when I had to get from a remote village high in the mountains to my lodgings in the valley below. I telephoned for a local taxi and within minutes an old, tiny Eastern European car arrived driven by a huge driver who had to sit across the two front seats to fit in the vehicle. I'm not small myself, and between the two of us the car was completely filled with flesh. Our combined weight was too much for the suspension, collapsing it to the point where the tops of the wheel arches touched the tyres. In this state the driver turned the vehicle and pointed it down the steep mountain road. Once he had lined the car up he slipped it out of gear to save petrol and off we went, freewheeling down the narrow mountain road. The two of us hurtled down as though we were entrants in the Great Cresta toboggan run; every time we came to a bend, the car threatened to flip over the edge of the mountain. The driver hardly touched his brakes, relying on our combined weight to slow the vehicle by the pressure of the wheel arches on the tyres. It certainly worked to slow the vehicle a little on the bends – the screaming tyres, clouds of blue smoke and smell of burning rubber were testament to this.

What this journey taught me was that I should have read the early signs when the taxi first arrived to collect me. The condition of the car and driver clearly demonstrated the dangers, but I had totally missed the signs: make sure *you* don't!

The second dangerous taxi ride I experienced was when I was working in India. I was staying in Pune and had to go to Mumbai (Bombay). Although I would have preferred to travel by train, there wasn't a convenient one to take, so I ordered a local taxi instead. Now, if you have ever been to India, you will know how dangerous it is to travel by car even for short journeys through cities.

I was hoping that the main highways were better organized, but they weren't. I spent five hours speeding along an absolutely packed narrow road so full of traffic that the taxi driver would often leave the road altogether and use the dusty vehicle-rutted roadside where whole families were living in tiny makeshift huts constructed from the wreckage of multiple vehicle crashes and empty cement bags. If the track was busy or there was a tree or dead cow blocking the way, the driver would swerve back onto the road in front of the following traffic, choose a small gap in the oncoming traffic and go straight across to the track on the opposite side of the road. These manoeuvres would have been bad enough had we been the only vehicle doing this, but we were only one of dozens doing the same – horrific!

I tried to talk some sense into the driver, but to no avail. In the end I decided that he drove in these conditions every day of his life, and that it was actually safer in the circumstances. Likewise, I believe that if you drive yourself in these situations, then you would have to drive in the same way to keep ahead of the game.

Avoid using taxis and other communal transport that is not subject to official checks on vehicles and their operators. Official taxis usually have a driver-licensing policy that goes some way toward checking the driver's competence to drive the vehicle and his honesty.

Trains

As in many other countries, the population of India uses rail travel extensively. Unfortunately, cooking aboard the trains is also allowed, and this is usually carried out on open stoves using butane gas – a very dangerous procedure in a train compartment, with no thought to safety.

If you do travel by train in these regions, sit as near as possible to the engine – and certainly on the engine side of any open-stove cooking: because of the train's direction of travel, the fire will not spread forward. If the train has an emergency alarm system fitted (unfortunately, not all do), try to sit near to it.

Sitting in the first carriage following the engine and in reach of the alarm should be your preferred position on all trains – both above-ground and underground – if it is late at night or isolated. It's bad enough waiting around on deserted stations for the train in the first place, without putting yourself in an even more vulnerable position by sitting in a deserted carriage a long way from the driver. If you cannot avoid travelling alone, plan your journeys at times of the day when the trains and stations are going to be full of people.

Where trains are properly supervised and there is no risk of fire, then you are probably safer if you sit towards the rear of the train, two or three carriages from the end: in the event of a train crash, the chances are that the impact will be taken by the engine and/or front carriages, so you will stand a better chance of survival in this position. On the same subject, if you are sitting with your back to the engine, then any impact at the front will force you into the relative safety of your seat – as opposed to catapulting you down the carriage if you were facing the front. If you do sit with your back to the engine, it's better if the seat opposite you is vacant, as this will keep you from being injured by a fellow passenger being catapulted from this position.

31. Air and Sea

Both in the air and at sea, you place a great deal of your safety and some of your control in the hands of the crew. There is not a lot you can do to influence their decisions unless you are an experienced pilot or ship's captain. What you can do is to make sure that you take notice of the emergency procedures as explained by the crew. You should also take the time to read the emergency procedure information that is supplied.

Aircraft

On aircraft, you are allowed to carry hand luggage, which may be the only opportunity for you to keep a few survival aids with you in case you need them. A simple survival kit should include the following items:

- Waterproofed matches and striker strip
- A small candle – the night-light type are ideal
- A ball of cotton wool to use as tinder
- A snare
- Water purifying tablets
- Condom (to use as a water carrier)
- Pencil and paper.

Many of the world's airlines serve alcohol on board, but from a survival point of view, life and alcohol do not mix. Having a gin and tonic may seem like a good idea, but even a little alcohol can impair your judgement. If there is an emergency, the last thing you want is to be too intoxicated to effect a successful evacuation – drinking water is a much safer option and, especially on long-haul flights, you will feel a lot fresher when you arrive at your destination.

If a fellow passenger is drinking heavily, monitor where they are all the time throughout the flight. Once again, if you need to act quickly to clear the aircraft, you don't want to be held up by an incapable drunk.

When you are sitting in one position for many hours, your muscles become relaxed and stiffen. Throughout the flight take the opportunity to walk the length of the plane or, if this is not possible, use simple muscle-movement exercises to keep the blood flowing. This will not only help to keep you alert in case of an emergency, but will also help to stop deep vein thrombosis (DVT).

Given the risk of terrorist attacks on aircraft and airports, always be on your guard. Keep an eye open for anyone who is acting suspiciously or is agitated. At the same time, keep a look-out for suspicious packages, or vehicles parked in restricted areas. Whenever you feel uncomfortable with a person or situation, bring it to the attention of security staff. Do not worry about the consequences of reporting something that turns out to be an innocent action. The fact is that you can never be too careful, and the detection of terrorists and terrorism is not just the responsibility of the security forces: it's the responsibility of all of us!

Where a terrorist or violent person is tackled on an aeroplane, leave this to people who are in close proximity to the person in question. Quite often, too many people get involved and fall over one another in the tightness of the plane's interior, allowing the perpetrator enough room to manoeuvre and to operate any equipment or weapons. If you are the closest, grab the person and restrict his/her movements by bear-hugging them, or use the strangle-hold explained in the *Self-Defence* section.

Ships

As with aircraft, you should take note of the emergency procedures as demonstrated by the crew. If you have a cabin, you must make sure that you find the quickest way to the deck, and can remember the route without having to stop and think about it. You will be allocated an emergency muster point, which you should remember and make your way to several times during the voyage. By doing this, you will not only remember the most efficient route to take, but can monitor any changes or obstacles that may appear subsequently. In your cabin, make sure that you keep warm, protective clothing by your door so that you can grab it in an emergency. Even in hot climates, if you have to evacuate the ship you will find that a lifeboat at sea can be both cold and wet. What you do not want is to be woken in the middle of the night and have to leave your cabin immediately without adequate clothing – staying behind after the emergency signal and searching your luggage for outdoor clothes will lessen your chances of survival. It will help you if you keep a small store of simple non-perishable food such as boiled sweets in your emergency clothing pockets. A small survival kit, such as the one mentioned in the *Aircraft* section above, should also be kept with your clothing.

Survival is about proper preparation. Prepare well in advance, and you will have the best chance of living through the ordeal.

Once you have evacuated the ship and have taken to a lifeboat, pay attention to the vessel's senior member, who will be an experienced member of the ship's crew. If there is no member of the ship's company aboard, there will be an instruction booklet, along with fresh water and emergency rations stowed in the boat. As soon as you board the lifeboat, make every effort to steer it away from the ship. Once you are a safe distance away, have your emergency signal equipment ready for immediate use, and attend to any injuries that you or your fellow survivors may have. Having completed this task, read the emergency booklet and plan your future action. Unless you are absolutely sure that no international emergency signal has been sent, stay in the area of the wreckage; the ship's radio operator will have signalled the position to the rescuers, and there will also be automatically operated equipment that sends out radio distress signals when it comes into contact with seawater. If there are other lifeboats in the area, join up with them to make as large a platform as possible. This will ensure that you can share the experience of others, help to protect everyone from capsizing, and help the rescuers to see you; all you have to do then is wait until the rescuers reach you.

If you have moved away from the site, head for land (see the *Search and Rescue* section). If you are unsure as to which direction any land is in, look for clouds building in an otherwise clear sky: clouds build over land. If there is bird life around, then you must also be relatively close to land, as no birds live solely on the sea and they must return to land to breed and roost. Early in the morning birds will fly away from land, whereas late in the afternoon and evening they will be returning to land.

32. Natural Disasters

Avalanche

I have never been caught in an avalanche, but I have seen one from a distance when I was working in the Bavarian Alps.

Avalanches are unpredictable, but should always be expected in snow-covered mountain areas. There are several ways in which an avalanche can occur. Loud noises are a major cause, and this is particularly dangerous when search-and-rescue aircraft are flying in the vicinity. Falling rocks or high winds can also start the movement of large areas of unstable snow and ice. Snow becomes very unstable when there is a quick thaw, or after a heavy snowfall when the new snow builds a deep layer on top of old compacted snow and is then disturbed and slides away, cascading down the mountain.

If you are travelling in areas that are prone to avalanches, be aware of thawing conditions, high winds, sudden heavy snowfalls and rain. If you have to travel in these conditions, keep away from steep faces, gullies and overhanging snow masses.

If, however, you are unfortunate enough to get caught in an avalanche, quickly discard any equipment such as skis, snowshoes or luggage you are carrying, as these will hamper your movements. If you can, move to the outer edges of the avalanche, where the force will be relatively less. When you are hit by the wall of snow, force yourself on top of it – rather like surfing a wave – lie as flat as you can and try to stay on top: using swimming strokes will help you to do this. As the avalanche comes to a halt, cover your nose and mouth by cupping your hands – this creates an air space. When the avalanche stops, use your hands to dig as large a space as possible around you before the snow freezes. If you can't get out, keep still in order to conserve your energy and oxygen until help arrives.

Volcanoes

Volcano eruptions are generally predictable. However, there are occasions when one erupts without warning or is in such a location that people have nowhere to go to escape it. You may well be caught up in either of these situations, and will have to do the best you can to survive.

Where a volcano erupts with force, a large quantity of very hot lava will be thrown out of it. If you are within the area of its fallout, you should get under cover – this may be in the cellars of buildings, under rock overhangs or any other place that protects you from falling hazards. Avoid getting under vehicles, as these may well catch fire and explode. Cover your mouth and nose with a scarf or handkerchief, and breathe through your nose only to cut down on the inhalation of gases and dust.

After the initial eruption, the volcano may continue to spew molten rock that creates a lava flow. This rarely moves at a great speed, but can still move sufficiently quickly to catch people out. So keep moving away from the flow.

Even after the flow has come to a halt and the lava solidifies, do not climb on or over it as the inner lava takes a long time to cool properly. The surface may look and feel hard enough to walk on, but you can fall through and be horribly burnt. Likewise, there is still a danger of poisonous gases for some considerable time after the initial blow.

33. Escape and Evasion

Life and people can never be underestimated. Both will take you by surprise when you least expect it. Although it may seem unlikely that you would ever need to use escape-and-evasion skills to survive, you never know. As a part of your overall survival, you may well need to evade a pursuer or escape from detention so that you can reach a safe place or meet up with people who can help you.

Having effected an escape, the last thing you want is to be captured again. Once you have cleared the immediate vicinity, choose an area that gives you good cover. Keep moving for as long as you can, watching your back trail as well as your forward route. Moving around in all locations creates noise, so take care to move deliberately, and avoid fast jerky movements, which will draw attention to your position – easy, flowing movements are not so easily seen. If your route takes you through dense undergrowth or an area where the human form is alien, break up your body shape and facial features – using camouflage made from vegetation and other material in the locality will help you to stay hidden. Tying local vegetation to your clothing and applying crushed berries and mud on your face and hands does not take long, and will create good camouflage.

Hiding by day and moving by night may well help you to evade capture, but moving in unfamiliar territory in the dark is not an easy option. When you do move, keep off local paths, roads and highways, as these will be in constant use. If you have to cross open ground, keep to the edges; do not walk in the open or across crop fields, deserts or snow even at night, as your tracks can easily be seen from the air. If possible, walk near to flowing water – using the noise this type of feature makes may give you the opportunity to move very quickly without being heard. Do not walk on exposed ridges or over the top of hills, as you will easily be seen against the sky. Change your course as often as possible, and climb through rock falls and over hard ground to mask your tracks. Keep away from local dwellings, as these may contain dogs that can hear you and alert the residents with their barking.

If you consider that dogs may be used to track you, walk in streams or through fields that contain stock such as cattle. Where you know tracker-dogs are going to be used, be prepared for a dog attack: carry a stout short log to use as a cosh in your strongest hand, and wrap spare clothing around your weaker forearm. If a dog does attack, offer it the protected forearm and, once the dog has grasped it, hit the dog at the back of the neck with the club: this blow should be made with sufficient force to break the dog's neck and kill it.

PART 7
Self-Help

34. First Aid

We should all have some knowledge of basic first-aid, as it is useful not only in a survival situation, but also in our everyday lives. The following information is included in order to give you a taste of the essentials, but I strongly recommend that you attend one of the many courses set up to teach the subject professionally.

In the first instance, you will have to decide which of the injured require the most attention – a difficult decision, as in a plane crash, for example, the injuries are going to be many and horrific. In all situations, your priorities as a first-aider are:

1. Keep the casualty alive
2. Stop the harmful condition from getting worse
3. Aid eventual recovery
4. Relieve suffering.

First-Aid Kits

Outdoor-activity and travel shops stock a wide range of first-aid kits especially suitable for the traveller. The type and size you need depend on the extent of your travel, the type of activities you are planning to undertake, your carrying capacity and the number of people involved. To these you can add medicines specific to your geographical location, and any personal medication.

Kits can be heavy and bulky, so bear this in mind when purchasing or assembling your own. On small expeditions, individual medical kits that include personal medication are better than a single, communal one. When you are carrying personal medication, make sure that the other members of the group know what it is and how to administer it, as well as any possible side-effects.

The golden rule when choosing your kit is to keep it simple. On all my trips, no matter how small, I carry the following:

- Several large squares of lint
- Bandages in various widths
- Sticking plasters (moleskin for blisters)
- Several extra-large plasters
- A roll of surgical tape
- Cotton-wool
- Safety pins
- Tube of antiseptic cream
- Bicarbonate of soda
- Scissors.

Always check that your kit is serviceable before departure – a lesson I learnt on one expedition at my female colleague's expense, when on a long-distance trek she complained of aching and sore shoulders. I opened my kit and took out a cream that had been in there for a number of years but never used. It had been sold for the very problem she was experiencing, but when I applied it to her shoulders they began to glow a lovely shade of crimson, shortly followed by blistering. Luckily there was a river nearby where she could cool off, although this was not really the best action to take, as had the blisters had burst, the dirty waters could have created a nasty infection. However, in the circumstances we had no alternative as she still had a heavy pack to carry for many more miles.

Procedure in the event of an accident

After the initial shock of the accident, you need to be able to follow a set routine. This minimizes the risk of poor decision-making, and allows you to carry on quickly with the job in hand. The recognized procedure is:

1. Carry out immediate first-aid
2. Never leave any injured or exhausted person alone
3. Keep casualties warm and comfortable
4. Regularly reassure the patient and other members of the group.

Breathing stopped

This eventuality obviously needs immediate action. Once you are satisfied that a person has actually stopped breathing, carry out the following procedure immediately (any time lost will result in permanent brain damage due to the lack of oxygen to this vital organ):

a) Place the casualty on his back, insulating him from the ground. Check the mouth, nose and throat, and clear if necessary. If the throat is blocked, roll the patient on his side and give a sharp slap between the shoulder blades. If this is impracticable because of his position or contra-indications, use the index finger to clear the obstruction.

b) Approaching the casualty from the side, pull up the lower jaw, holding your free hand under the patient's neck so that the head is tilting back and the neck is stretched to allow the free passage of air to the lungs. Check that the tongue is not blocking the airway.

MOUTH TO MOUTH

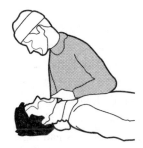

Clear the airway before attempting mouth-to-mouth resuscitation.

c) While holding the back of the neck as described, pinch the patient's nostrils shut with the thumb and forefinger of your other hand, then remove the hand supporting the neck and pull the lower jaw open, making sure that the neck remains uppermost and stretched.

d) Seal the casualty's mouth with yours, and blow air into the mouth approximately every four seconds (you may feel more comfortable with this procedure if you use a piece of open woven cloth, such as your handkerchief, as a means of protection between you and the patient, or you may wish to purchase a ready-made aid for your first-aid kit). Release the seal on the mouth and turn your head to the side when taking fresh air, as this stops you inhaling carbon dioxide being exhaled from the patient's mouth. It is most important that you take a normal breath, as constantly taking large amounts of air may hyperventilate you. Continue this procedure until the patient's chest rises spontaneously and there is the sound of air leaving the mouth. Allow the casualty to resume breathing unaided.

e) Continue to check that the tongue is not blocking the airway.

f) The throat may become blocked during this procedure, with vomit or blood stopping the air from reaching the lungs. Slapping the patient between the shoulder blades as before should clear this. Wipe the throat, clear the mouth and resume blowing.

g) Keep the casualty warm, and after he has revived treat him as a stretcher-case no matter how well he feels. He should be placed in the recovery position.

RECOVERY POSITION

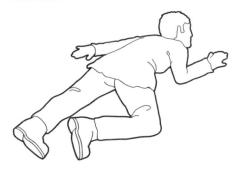

Keeping the patient in this position will lessen the chances of the patient choking on vomit.

Heart stopped (external chest compression)

a) You may find that the casualty is unconscious, and that at first glance he does not appear to be breathing.

b) Stop and consider the cause. Check the heart beat by taking the pulse; if no pulse is present, then the heart has stopped beating and immediate action is required. It is important that you keep the blood circulating around the body to supply the vital organs. This can be done by external cardiac massage as detailed below.

c) Place the casualty on their back on a flat, hard surface. Locate the lower part of the breastbone (the bony part of the centre of the chest, just above the stomach); place the heel of your hand over the bone and the heel of your other hand over the first; interlock the fingers, making sure the palms and fingers are well clear of the patient's chest – only the heel of the hand should be in contact with the body.

d) Keeping your arms straight and locked at the elbows, rock forward, firmly pressing down on the chest bone; you should repeat this pumping action approximately every second. Keep the pressure steady and controlled, avoiding sudden jerking.

The above procedure pumps blood around the body to the vital organs. However, blood alone will not be sufficient, as it needs to be oxygenated, which involves mouth-to-mouth breathing as described above. You should combine the two procedures in the following way: give five chest compressions, followed by one breath; repeat until the casualty revives, or professional help arrives.

REMEMBER
a) Place the heel of the hand over the lower part of the breastbone
b) Place the heel of the other hand over the first (keep palms and fingers off the body)
c) Rock forwards (straight arms) five times
d) Give one mouth-to-mouth breath
e) Return to (a) above for as long as you can
f) When breathing and heartbeat are both present, check for spinal injury; if none is present, put the patient in the recovery position.

No matter how good the recovery is, treat the patient as a stretcher-case and evacuate him to hospital as soon as the situation allows. Keep checking that the casualty is not vomiting – if so, keep the airway clear.

Unconsciousness

This condition covers everything from a faint to a complete coma. Causes of unconsciousness can include lack of food, low blood pressure, loss of blood, a blow to the head and severe injury. You should view all cases with concern: always put the casualty in the recovery position, and check for breathing and pulse.

Do not: Place a pillow under the head
But do: Send for help
           Loosen clothing, especially around the waist and neck
           Check that the airway is clear: vomit kills
           Remember to keep the casualty in the recovery position, which allows the vomit to spew out, keeping the patient from inhaling it; an unconscious patient may be unable to swallow.

Bleeding

Do not use a tourniquet for this condition. I was once informed that more men lost limbs from the misuse of tourniquets during the First World War than from any type of war wound. A tourniquet restricts the flow of blood to tissue, which causes the tissue to die, resulting in gangrene which, in turn, results in the eventual amputation of the limb – if you are lucky – and death if you are not!

Heavy pressure directly over the wound will stop 99% of bleeding. If blood is spurting out, apply thumb or finger pressure down onto the wound and keep it there.

Shock

This condition is defined as a state of prostration that is found in injured persons. There is some degree of shock in all cases of injury – no matter how slight. The symptoms to look for are listed below, but they will not all be present, however, any two should be sign enough for you to act:

Shallow, irregular breathing
Weak, rapid pulse
Cold and clammy skin
Extreme pallor usually, but in some cases the skin appears bluish
or even flushed
Dilated pupils (unusually large)
Thirst
Nausea
Weakness, fainting, dizziness
Lack of awareness or even unconsciousness.

You must: Keep the patient warm and comfortable, but avoid overheating
Give warm, sweet drinks – unless the patient has injuries that would require hospitalization
Relieve pain by giving analgesics, but not if the patient is unconscious or showing contra-indications, such as internal bleeding or a head injury
Give regular reassurance throughout the recovery
Keep the patient's feet slightly higher than his head.

Exposure and exhaustion

Exposure is a severe chilling of the body surface, causing a progressive fall of body temperature with the risk of death from hypothermia-deficient body heat.

Physical exhaustion is an additional factor over and above the deficiency of body heat that kills quickly. You must be constantly on the look-out for exhaustion in your group. In the majority of fatalities (as a result of the above), it has been impossible to separate the effects of one from the other.

Symptoms:

It is very difficult to determine the early stages of mild exposure and exhaustion. You must constantly be on the look-out for any of the following signs:

Complaints of feeling cold, tired or listless

Unexpected or unreasonable behaviour

Sudden, uncontrollable shivering

Physical or mental lethargy, which includes a failure to respond to, or understand questions or orders

Slowing-down or stumbling

Disturbed or failed vision

Violent outbursts of energy or speech

Slurring speech

Collapse, stupor or unconsciousness.

The following factors will aggravate the symptoms, and must be eliminated before recovery can take place:

Soaked clothing, especially with high winds

General chilling from low air temperatures

Immersion in water, which has a high conductivity of body heat

Immobility due to injury will reduce the patient's ability to generate heat

A combination of fatigue, anxiety, cold and mental stress is extremely dangerous

Unusual thinness

Alcoholic beverages.

Take note: the elements are potentially lethal – give them the respect they deserve.

A thorough knowledge of the symptoms, first-aid and an understanding of 'wind chill' will all help, but above all prevention is better than cure.

During my military career, I was taught the 'Buddy Buddy' system, and I have yet to find anything that works as well; this is where men are paired off to watch over each other at all times. By adopting this method, the early symptoms of exposure and exhaustion can be recognized and action taken before reaching the stage at which injury and death occur.

Another good military teaching is the mnemonic, 'cold feet': it is a memory-aid checklist for prevention against the cold.

C – Clean clothing.
O – Overheating is out.
L – Loose layers only.
D – Dryness demanded.

F – Face, finger, face, exercises.
E – Equipment checked and serviceable.
E – Eat your rations.
T – Tight boots are terrible.

In an emergency, your first-aid should be as follows:
1. Prevent further heat loss. Put the casualty into a sleeping, plastic, bivvy or survival bag, ensuring that he is well insulated from the ground and from the sides, including head and face (a balaclava is ideal).
2. Get his companion into the bag with him to supply body heat.
3. Protect both of them from the elements.
4. Get the rest of the party working to erect a shelter over them or construct a windbreak. This also helps the remainder of the party to keep warm.
5. Watch the casualty to check that their breathing or pulse does not stop. In either case, resuscitation and/or external cardiac massage must be started immediately.
6. As soon as possible, brew up, ensuring everyone in the party has something warm to drink and something to eat.

7. In all cases of accident or emergency you should send for help, but before the messengers are sent out, make sure that they have rested, had a drink, are not suffering from exhaustion, and are capable of safely carrying out the task: you must not put others at risk.

8. Once again, the casualty must be treated as a stretcher-case – no matter how well he recovers.

Frostbite

1. Frostbite occurs when the body tissue freezes: this is not until a skin temperature of -1°C is reached. The timescale depends on the severity of the cold air, wind speed, the area of flesh exposed and the amount of blood constriction.

2. Minor frostbite mostly affects the body's extremities, such as the nose, cheeks, ears and fingers. This is partly due to the difficulty of insulating these areas sufficiently, but also because of the body's defence mechanism. As the body becomes colder, the blood supply restricts itself to the body core in an effort to preserve inner body heat. Severe frostbite occurs mainly in the feet – the location and shape of the feet make it particularly difficult to insulate them against heat loss, and tight footwear is another contributory factor.

There is a well-proven procedure that will prevent frostbitten feet. Simply remove footwear and socks and massage the feet for 10–15 minutes (do not rub them, as your skin will be extremely fragile at this stage). Do this often, and you will not get frostbite. Always keep a spare pair of dry socks next to your skin (I usually keep mine around my stomach) to change into, and change your socks at least once daily. When you bed down, remove your footwear and massage your feet. Avoid sleeping with your footwear on, but if you have no alternative, make sure the laces are undone and the footwear is slack fitting.

Should you suffer from frostbite, then the following action should aid recovery:

a) The affected parts will become painful: this should be sufficient warning, and you should warm them immediately. At this stage, cover the affected parts and get into some form of shelter. Use the 'Buddy Buddy' system: place feet, ears and nose against your mate's skin. A number of years ago, I went down with mild frostbite in the Bavarian Alps: ever since then, the slightest amount of exposure to cold wind or water causes the blood supply to my fingers to give up the struggle. My fingers turn waxy-white without my noticing, and it is only when I have stuck them under my friend's armpits and the blood begins to return that I feel pain. It's at times like these that you find out who your mates really are! If these symptoms occur when you are alone, use the naturally warmer parts of your own body to warm them. In both cases, keep the rest of the body well insulated from the cold. Once the pain ceases and normal sensations return, the danger is over.

b) Some people may be so pre-occupied or stunned with cold and exhaustion that they do not notice the pain. Eventually this pain subsides as the area becomes numb. When this occurs, the affected area takes on the waxy-white appearance I have described, and it becomes quite hard to the touch. This stage is serious, and action must be taken immediately to stop the condition from spreading and becoming worse. Shelter must be found and re-warming carried out immediately. The affected tissue is already damaged, and rubbing it must be avoided at all costs, as this only makes the situation worse. Rapid warming in water at a temperature of 42–43°C proves to be the best treatment. In a survival situation, you may have to make do with wrapping the affected area in damp clothes using tepid water, or body-warmed underclothing donated by the stronger members of the group.

Broken bones

If conscious, the casualty will complain of pain and will usually be unable to move the injured part properly. A broken limb may look mis-shapen, and swelling and bruising may be present caused by internal bleeding flooding the injury. The casualty may also complain of extreme tenderness over the break.

Even if you only vaguely suspect a break, treat it as one: you will be better safe than sorry.

The following action should be taken:

1. Immobilize the break, which will stop the situation from becoming worse: immobilization prevents the broken bones from rubbing together. Where possible, use a splint, otherwise immobilize the affected limb against the casualty's body.
2. Pad the limb, particularly between the legs, with anything that is handy.
3. Bind the splint and broken area firmly, but not too tightly. Broken

limbs swell and tight bindings restrict free blood flow. Pins and needles, and a deadening of the limb, are signs of too tight a binding.

If you suspect a broken back, move the casualty as little as possible, making sure that he is always well-supported.

Remember, nothing is impossible as long as the will to survive is present.

Death

Regrettably, some accidents do result in death. Do not be too ready to assume death, but carry on with resuscitation for as long as possible. A dead person has no pulse, no breath and no response; after a while the body will chill. If this state is finally accepted, move everyone away from the body and cover it. As soon as possible, sit down and write down as much information as possible about how the person died: an enquiry will be held sooner or later, and your notes will be of great use. Other members of the group may be upset at the death, and you should busy yourself by attending to them. Death is an inevitable part of living, and overreaction to it only makes the situation worse.

Although I have already mentioned cannibalism in an earlier section of this book, I think it is worth reiterating the dilemma here. In the fight for life, many a survivor has lived by eating a dead person. This action is shunned by the majority of civilized people but, faced with the prospect of death by starvation, I believe that few of us would not eventually eat another who, after all, was dead and therefore unaware of the situation. If you did not eat and subsequently died, then this would be a waste of two lives, not one – I for one would expect to be eaten if my body was lying there doing nothing.

Long-term medical problems

After the initial first-aid, medical problems will inevitably arise during the fight for survival; obviously, these will become greater with the passage of time. Personal and communal hygiene should be attended to from day one, as it is in this area that most long-term problems will arise. Most diseases, especially in the tropics, are water-borne; always make sure that water is purified using one of the methods explained in the section on *Water*. In warm, tropical climates, ailments caused by the sun will be the first problems to emerge, especially when the group is working to develop a comfortable camp. Once again, prevention is better than cure, and that starts with recognizing the symptoms of the more common ailments.

Sunburn

This is the reddening and eventual blistering of the skin due to the sun's ultra-violet rays. Symptoms include:

- Pain from burning
- Temporarily upset stomach
- Headache
- Fever
- Occasional vomiting
- The body's natural ability to regulate heat may be reduced because the affected areas are unable to sweat.

There is no quick cure available. Skin needs to develop a protective tan. In regions where the sun is very strong, exposure to it must be no longer than five minutes on the first day, gradually allowing more exposure as the days pass.

Prickly heat

This is very common, especially in the tropics. The prickly sensation is very annoying, and plays havoc with sleep patterns. It is caused by blocking of the sweat glands, thus impairing the body's ability by sweating to cool. The sufferer must be kept in the shade, constantly removed from any heat stress, and regularly washed with purified water.

Heat exhaustion

There are four separate conditions – all of which are serious – and left alone the sufferer will possibly die. These are:

1. Anhidrotic heat exhaustion (anhidrotic meaning without perspiration). Symptoms include:

- The inability to sweat
- Severe prickly heat
- Loss of energy
- Lack of initiative and interest.

This type of disorder is the most difficult to treat, as the sufferer does not possess the capacity to cool the body by sweating. This will cause severe dehydration – a condition from which he may die. Make every effort to keep him cool, administering plenty of fluids.

2. Salt-deficient heat exhaustion. This can occur after two to three days of heavy sweating without sufficient salt replacement. Symptoms include:

- Heavy sweating
- Nausea
- Vomiting (not always present)
- Muscle cramps (which may involve the large muscle groups, and morphine may have to be used to relieve the severe pain)
- Pallor
- Collapse.

The sufferer is in a potentially lethal situation. Rest and plenty of liquids plus salt tablets must be administered and, where possible, immediate evacuation to medical aid should be arranged. Do not give salt in water, as vomiting at this stage will be lethal.

3. Water-deficient heat exhaustion. This usually follows periods of heavy sweating with restricted water intake. Symptoms include:

- Complaints of vague discomfort.
- No appetite
- Dizziness
- Impatience
- Weariness
- Sleepiness
- Tingling sensation
- Shortage of breath
- Blue tinge to the skin
- Difficulty in walking.

Eventually, the victim will be unable to stand or control his muscles, and hysteria and/or delirium follow. Reassurance, rest, shade and an ample supply of water promote a rapid recovery.

4. Heat hyperprexia and heat-stroke. Those affected will be struck down rapidly and die; therefore these are potentially the most dangerous of the heat disorders.

Heat hyperprexia is a high fever defined by a body temperature of 41°C or more. Heat-stroke is the failure of the body's heat-regulating mechanism. With heat hyperprexia, the body's heat regulating becomes impaired, resulting in a rapid progression to heat-stroke. The body temperature steadily rises in the absence of sweating, and death ensues at a temperature of approximately 43°C.

Heat-stroke

Symptoms: the onset is sudden, with the victim showing no signs of distress even a few hours previously. The disturbances are profound:
- Delirium
- Convulsions
- Partial or complete loss of consciousness
- Snoring breathing
- Hot, dry, flushed skin.

The only cure is the immediate cooling of the body to check the rise in temperature. A delay of as little as two hours in this process can mean the difference between life and death.

Treatment:
1. Remove the victim from direct sunlight.
2. Strip him of his clothing.
3. Wrap him in a wet sheet or towel (the water should be only a couple of degrees cooler than the patient's body temperature).
4. Fan him to promote cooling by evaporation.
5. You must not apply iced water, as this does not have the desired effect.
6. Start the treatment as soon as you suspect heat-stroke.

There is a tendency for a victim of heat-stroke to crawl into a shaded area, where he may escape notice during the critical period; always be on the look out for this.

I have dealt here with the majority of heat disorders – most of which can be overcome if you are aware of them from the start. Water plays a big part in the prevention and treatment of them all.

Local medical hazards

Jungle: a possible medical hazard list is as follows:

a) Poisoning by eating or contact with vegetation
b) Malaria, dysentery, sand-fly fever and typhus
c) All animal life
d) Sun and heat.

Once again, prevention is better than cure.

This is especially true of jungle diseases with which you could come in contact. I have never heard of anyone dying from a disease against which he was inoculated, or for which he had had the appropriate medication before entering an infested zone. Prior to any proposed trip, check not only which areas you will be visiting, but also the areas over which you will be flying.

I have had the opportunity of travelling on the flight-deck of a number of aircraft. Unbeknown to the majority of the passengers on civil aircraft, the pilots are continually monitoring the course and plotting possible escape routes and emergency-landing facilities: if anything goes wrong, the pilots will readily divert to the nearest or safest airfield. This could be anywhere, so do make sure that you are fully inoculated and have the correct medication for the zones you travel through as well as your ultimate destination.

Malaria

This disease is caused by a bite from an infected mosquito. The sufferer begins by feeling chilly, usually followed by shivering; the next stage is hot and cold fevers alternating throughout the illness. Rest and copious quantities of water to drink with six to eight mepacrine tablets per day should help until the patient's temperature drops. Even after this there will be some recurrence.

Sand-fly fever

This is caused by the bite of the sand fly, and symptoms and treatment are similar to those for malaria. In both of the above cases, the following precautions will help:

1) Where possible, keep away from potential infected areas. In the case of mosquitoes, these will be swampy areas. The sand fly favours areas by rivers in forest clearings and by the seashore. A smoky fire tends to keep them at bay, but even with the smokiest of fires the insects still manage to get through. The wearing of long-sleeved coats and trousers helps.

2) Whenever possible, construct mosquito nets and regularly spray the inside of them with an anti-insect spray. If in more temperate zones you are troubled by midges, the following concoctions will help:

- Pine bark (*Pinus*), crushed into a pulp makes a good repellent.
- Elderberry (*Sambucus nigra*). Bruise some leaves and wear a sprig of them around your person; note that the green parts of this plant are poisonous.
- Fleabanes (*Conyza*). Picked and set to smoulder, these can delouse the most inaccessible areas of your shelter, but once again beware, as these are poisonous to humans.
- Fly Agaric (*Amanita muscaria*). An infusion of 1 kg to 2 litres painted around the area of your camp will further help to keep at bay any insect life. Be careful, however, as this is a very potent poison and must not be eaten under any circumstances.

Dysentery

This is caused by eating or drinking polluted food or water. The symptoms are severe swelling of the bowels, resulting in stomach pains and continuous diarrhoea; the faeces will be green and bloody. If you are lucky, you can treat it with sulphaguandadine. Other than this the only aid is to give the patient plenty of well-boiled water and a diet of soft food and liquids, such as boiled milk, boiled rice, coconut milk or boiled bread.

Diarrhoea

This condition is very common in a survival situation because of the type of food you will be forced to eat. Diarrhoea is not to be taken lightly, as it is a source of infection to all that are in the location, and will cause severe dehydration to anyone suffering from it. Personal hygiene will keep it at bay. Treat it by resting, and drink unlimited amounts of fluid (boiled, of course). If you have any available to you, use kaolin powder – a natural alternative is peeled and grated apple, but wait until the apple turns brown (pectin) before eating it.

I was once told by an experienced expedition doctor of a 'kill or cure' remedy called the Everest Blunderbuss Cocktail. Apparently, shortly after taking it you fall fast asleep, and then awake to a bout of constipation that will last for up to six days. The recipe for this very potent brew is:

4–6 drops of tincture of morphine

2 tablets of codeine phosphate

2 tablespoons of kaolin powder

4 tablets of diphenoxylate (Lomotil).

Constipation

Once again, this is not to be made fun of, as it can result in a more serious problem. As soon as the stools begin to be difficult to pass, drink plenty of liquid and supplement the diet with plenty of fruit and roughage. In cases of extreme – and I do mean extreme – constipation, give an enema by passing a pint of soapy solution up into the rectum, using a well-greased rubber tube. I cannot stress too much the importance of caution and the proper sterilization of equipment when this has to be undertaken.

While we are talking about the more unsavoury functions of the body, I feel it necessary to stress the importance of personal and communal hygiene. No one wants to live with a dirty person – except the least welcome friends such as lice and mites. Ticks are also a considerable menace and they may even swarm onto a person when disturbed. All of the above will have less effect if the body and clothing are washed regularly. The more persistent of these parasites may be dislodged by smoking – that is hanging your clothes or standing nude in the path of a very smoky fire. From time to time you may find leeches about your person; it is no use pulling them off, as all this does is detach the body from the jaws which are then left in the skin to cause an infection. When troubled by leeches, use a smouldering stick or cigarette to burn them off.

We have already mentioned the 'Buddy Buddy' system in colder regions; this system has its uses in warmer climates too. Each person should look after his mate and watch for any deterioration in his attitude and physical aptitude. They should help each other to wash properly and make sure that ablutions are performed regularly.

In locations where a static camp has been set up, a communal latrine should be dug, along with a rubbish trench.

Wild animals are going to present a further hazard, but you will usually hear or see them – in which case either you will keep away from them or they from you. The same applies to snakes: they, too, will leave you alone, as long as you do not disturb them. Unfortunately, they are less easy to see and you may accidentally disturb one. In the event of one of your group being bitten, the following action should be taken:

1) Reduce the spread of venom by restricting the blood flow on either side of the bite.
2) Keep the bitten area lower than the heart.
3) Wash the wound with soapy water.
4) Make every effort to evacuate the casualty to a hospital as soon as possible (if you can, kill the snake and take it with you to the hospital, as it will help doctors to administer the correct anti-venom serum).
5) Stop the victim from making any form of movement, as this will quicken the blood flow and force the venom around the body more quickly.
6) The pain must be treated, and reassurance given to the victim.
7) The cobra spits venom into the eyes: if this happens, wash the eyes with plenty of clean water.

35. World Danger Spots

No matter where you travel to in the world, there is always going to be a problem with crimes against the person. Keeping to the simple rules outlined in this book will help you to stay safe. The following is a short list of terrorist groups that are a threat to everyone who does not share their particular beliefs. Unfortunately, terrorists are indiscriminate in their siting of bombs and armed attacks. As a result, we are all vulnerable and can be caught up in violent situations. Understanding that the threat exists and keeping abreast of the latest terrorist groups, their methods and usual theatres of operation will help us to make informed decisions about our travel and business plans.

Before you travel, contact your own government foreign-affairs offices to seek their advice and to obtain the latest intelligence they have on the areas you intend to visit.

Afghanistan

Terrorist groups: IG, Islamic Group (Al-Gama'at al-Islamiyya), HUM (Harakat ul-Mujahidin), al-Jihad, al-Qaida and IMU (Islamic Movement of Uzbekistan).

Acts of terrorism: attacks on tourists, kidnapping and assassinations.

Algeria

Terrorist groups: GIA, (Armed Islamic Group).

Acts of terrorism: attacks on civilians and tourists, assassinations, bombings, kidnapping and hijackings.

Austria

Terrorist groups: IG, Islamic Group (Al-Gama'at al-Islamiyya).

Acts of terrorism: tourist attacks, kidnappings and assassinations.

Brazil

Terrorist groups: FARC (Revolutionary Armed Forces of Columbia).

Acts of terrorism: bombings, murders, hijackings and drug trafficking.

Columbia

Terrorist groups: ELN (National Liberation Army) and FARC (Revolutionary Armed Forces of Columbia).

Acts of terrorism: bombings, hijackings, kidnappings, attacks on tourists and murders.

Ecuador

Terrorist groups: FARC (Revolutionary Armed Forces of Columbia).

Acts of terrorism: bombings, attacks on tourists, kidnappings, and drug trafficking.

Egypt

Terrorist groups: IG Islamic Group (Al-Gama'at al-Islamiyya), al-Jihad.

Acts of terrorism: attacks on tourists, kidnappings and assassinations.

France

Terrorist groups: ETA (Basque Fatherland and Liberty).

Acts of terrorism: bombings, assassinations, kidnappings, robberies and extortion.

Greece

Terrorist groups: ELA (Revolutionary People's Struggle), 17 November (Revolutionary Organization 17 November).

Acts of terrorism: bombings and assassinations.

India

Terrorist groups: Sikh Terrorism; since September 11, there have been several attacks by Muslims on Christians attending religious services.

Acts of terrorism: tourist attacks, assassinations, bombings and kidnapping.

Iran

Terrorist groups: IMU (Islamic Movement of Uzbekistan).

Acts of terrorism: bombings and kidnapping.

Iraq

Terrorist groups: ANO (Abu Nidal organization) and PLF (Palestine Liberation Front).

Acts of terrorism: tourist attacks, hijacking and assassinations.

Irish Republic

Terrorist groups: CIRCA (Continuity Irish Republican Army), IRA (Irish Republican Army), LVF (Loyalist Volunteer Force), PIRA (Provisional Irish Republican Army) and RIRA (Real IRA).

Acts of terrorism: bombings, assassinations, extortion, robberies and kidnappings.

Israel

Terrorist groups: Kach and Kahane Chai, PIJ (The Palestine Islamic Jihad), PFLP (Popular Front for the Liberation of Palestine) and HAMAS (Islamic Resistance Movement).

Acts of terrorism: shootings, harassment and threats, suicide bombings and tourist attacks.

Jordan

Terrorist groups: PIJ (The Palestine Islamic Jihad).

Acts of terrorism: suicide bombings.

Kyrgyzstan

Terrorist groups: IMU (Islamic Movement of Uzbekistan).

Acts of terrorism: bombings and kidnapping.

Lebanon

Terrorist groups: ANO (Abu Nidal Organization), Hizballah (Party of God), JRA (Japanese Red Army), PIJ (The Palestine Islamic Jihad), PFLP (Popular Front for the Liberation of Palestine) and PFLP-GC (Popular Front for the Liberation of Palestine-General Command).

Acts of terrorism: bombings, tourist attacks, kidnapping and hijackings.

Libya

Terrorist groups: ABU (Abu Nidal organization).

Acts of terrorism: bombings, tourist attacks, hijacking and assassinations.

Pakistan

Terrorist groups: HUM (Harakat ul-Mujahidin) and Al-Jihad, Jamaat ul-Fuqra.

Acts of terrorism: kidnappings, tourist attacks, assassinations, fire bombings, murder and fraud.

Panama

Terrorist groups: FARC (Revolutionary Armed Forces of Columbia).

Acts of terrorism: bombings, murders, kidnappings, extortion and drug trafficking.

Peru

Terrorist groups: SL Shining Path (Sendero Luminoso).

Acts of terrorism: bombings and assassinations.

Philippines

Terrorist groups: ASG (Abu Sayyaf Group), ABB (Alex Boncayao Brigade) and NPA (New People's Army).

Acts of terrorism: bombings, assassinations, kidnappings, drug trafficking and tourist attacks.

Russian Federation

Terrorist groups: AUM (AUM Supreme Truth).

Acts of terrorism: tourist attacks.

South Africa

Terrorist groups: Pagad (Qibla and People against Gangsterism and Drugs).

Acts of terrorism: bombings and tourist attacks.

Spain

Terrorist groups: ETA (Basque Fatherland and Liberty).

Acts of terrorism: bombings, assassinations, kidnappings and tourist attacks.

Sri Lanka

Terrorist groups: LTTE (Liberation Tigers of Tamil Eelam).

Acts of terrorism: bombings and assassinations, although the LTTE has refrained from targeting Western tourists for fear of foreign governments cracking down on Tamil expatriates involved in fund-raising.

Sudan

Terrorist groups: ANO (Abu Nidal Organisation), al Jihad.

Acts of terrorism: tourist attacks, bombings and assassinations

Syria

Terrorist groups: ABU (Abu Nidal organisation), PIJ (The Palestine Islamic Jihad), PFLP (Popular Front for the Liberation of Palestine) and PFLP-GC (Popular Front for the Liberation of Palestine-General Command).

Acts of terrorism: tourist attacks, bombings and assassinations.

Tajikistan

Terrorist groups: IMU (Islamic Movement of Uzbekistan)

Acts of terrorism: bombings.

Turkey

Terrorist groups: PKK (Kurdistan Workers' Party), DHKP/C.

Acts of terrorism: tourist attacks, bombings, kidnapping and assassinations.

United Kingdom

Terrorist groups: IG Islamic Group (Al-Gama'at al-Islamiyya), al-Jihad, CIRCA (Continuity Irish Republican Army), IRA (Irish Republican Army), LVF (Loyalist Volunteer Force), OV (Orange Volunteers), RIRA (Real IRA), RHD (Red Hand Defenders) and PIRA (Provisional Irish Republican Army).

Acts of terrorism: tourist attacks, bombings, assassinations, kidnappings, extortion, robberies and arson.

United States of America

Terrorist groups: Party of God (Hizballah), Jamaat ul-Fuqra and Sikh Terrorism. Since September 11, there has been a great increase in terrorist activity in the USA. There is a threat from the majority of terrorist organizations whose members are – or who support – Islamic terrorists.

Acts of terrorism: bombings, kidnapping, tourist attacks, fire bombing, assassinations, murder and fraud.

Uzbekistan

Terrorist groups: IMU (Islamic Movement of Uzbekistan).

Acts of Terrorism: bombings, kidnapping and tourist attacks.

Venezuela

Terrorist groups: ELN (National Liberation Army) and FARC (Revolutionary Armed Forces of Columbia).

Acts of terrorism: kidnapping, hijacking, bombings, extortion, murders, drug trafficking and tourist attacks.